The Living ZODIAC

BLACK WATCH
New York

Published by Black Watch
under arrangenent with Ottenheimer Publishers Inc.
1632 Reistertown Road, Baltimore,
Maryland, 21208

Library of Congress Catalog Card Number 74 – 78298

ISBN 0 – 88486 – 003 – 5

Printed by Henri Proost, Turnhout, Belgium.

This edition not to be sold outside the U.S.A. or Canada

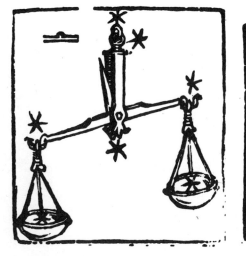
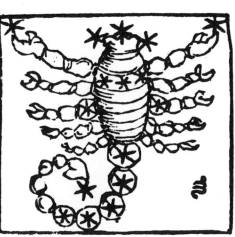

Introduction

Astrology is one of the oldest sciences known to man. Its fascination
has endured for well over 5000 years, and it still has much to teach
us today. Our planet Earth is only one tiny part of the cosmos, a
vital link in a living system of energy which pervades the universe.
The basic assumption of astrology is founded in the idea that every
element of the cosmos influences the whole, and that the structure
which we know as the Zodiac has particularly strong relevance to our
Earth. In *The Living Zodiac*, the author, Terence Higgins, has
examined in detail these spheres of influence, providing a clear-cut
account of how we are affected by the position and movement of the
planets. As well as being an exciting source of information for the
curious reader, *The Living Zodiac* is also a highly practical handbook
for the new student of astrology. Anyone who wishes to know how to
cast a horoscope is given complete instructions, step by step.

One of the most intriguing aspects of zodiac lore is the world of
correspondences – each sign of the zodiac has its own set of
references, animals, plants, special stones, individual characteristics
and talents. *The Living Zodiac* is packed with beautiful illustrations
of the correspondences, as well as dramatic new illustrations for each
of the zodiac signs. A must for stargazers of all persuasions, this is
both a delightful addition to your bookshelf, and a useful source of
reference to the budding astrologer.

Author: Terence Higgins
Editor: Yvonne Deutch
Design: Pedro Pra-Lopez
Cover: Peter Rauter
Zodiac Designs: Peter Jones/Trevor Goring

Contents

THE LIVING ZODIAC

A BRIEF HISTORY OF ASTROLOGY

Astrology is a practical, if not a precise, science that has existed for some 5,000 years from the time that man was first capable of logical thought processes. Since man first asked the questions 'What is life?' and 'What are we doing here?', astrology has been his constant companion frequently misleading, provoking, exasperating and completely bewildering, but always capable of producing the occasional shaft of enlightening reason and logic. Astrology is a venerable Methuselah, a royal art. The ancients taught that astrology was one of the keys to the many enigmas that plague man in his unceasing and unerring quest to determine what his role in the universe is, and this knowledge probably lingers on subconsciously, causing many millions of people to consult astrological forecasts in newspapers and magazines. Unfortunately these summaries (for at best they are but the briefest of generalisations) are a travesty of what astrology really is – proof of the degenerative and commercialising processes that befall us in an atomic age. Most scientific

Below: *The ancient science of astrology: two astrologers preparing a horoscope, from the section on the casting of horoscopes in Robert Fludd,* Utriusque Cosmi . . . Historia,

opinion, too, inclines to the view that astrology is an ancient and outdated Hermetic belief, to be carefully packaged and deposited in the catacombs of the museums alongside hostile neighbours such as Cabbalism, Alchemy and Ritual Magic. Neither of these attitudes are to be commended and indeed, are to be vehemently condemned.

It is perfectly obvious that mankind is not to be divided into twelve convenient groups, each member of which is to have his or her own completely identical character, which is what newspaper forecasts would imply. It is not so obvious that many of those who claim to be scientific experts and deny the validity of astrology out of hand, have made no apparent study of the subject – an oversight of gross intellectual negligence. The scientific experts who profess to know everything about the stars, counter the idea of the stars having an influence upon mankind with hostile and abrupt rejection. The astrologer, whose very existence is founded upon this belief, has fought for centuries to establish the reputation of astrology as a practical science. One that teaches the individual

how to use the information obtained from astrology as a means of adjusting his life-style to a more agreeable point of equilibrium. Astrologers and scientists have been locked in bitter conflict for centuries as to the authenticity of astrology. The battle is gradually subsiding with the discovery by scientists that there are close links between man and the solar system. We are in the middle of a scientific revolution and perhaps at a turning point in time, when 'precise' science will have to reconsider some of its fixed opinions with regard to the role astrology plays in the attempt to solve the age-old puzzle, 'What is life?'.

Astrology does not entail any form of psychism, occult or any other incidental phenomena but simply the processing and interpretation of selected data of mathematical and astronomical origin. Bearing in mind that our knowledge of astrology is far from complete,

Below: *Arabian astrologers, depicted here with highly complex instruments for scanning the heavens, were regarded as pioneers in the science of forecasting future events.*

Above: *Our version of the zodiac is derived from many sources; some traditional elements are recognizable in unusual forms in this Babylonian Zodiac.*

and is riddled with minor pitfalls, such as centuries of superstition, ignorance and antagonistic attitudes of science, the uses of astrology are manifold. It is, in essence, a practical science of superior quality, which can have many definitions ranging from Larousse's 'The Art of prediction of the future through observation of the stars', to the more reasonable 'Science of the effects of the solar system upon terrestrial life'. At any rate, astrology warrants an objective analysis and this we shall endeavour to do.

Astrology and the User

Most people are unaware that there is a distinct difference between the scientific subjects of astrology and astronomy. They are often mistakenly identified as being one and the same and 20th century education, in its ignorance, has done little or nothing to remove this misnomer. The words astrology and astronomy are derived from the Greek in the following way:

Astron: A star;
Logos: A reasoning, a science,
from which we get the name astrology.
Astron: A star;
Nomos: A law,

hence astronomy. We can therefore observe that astrology is concerned with the science of, or the meaning we can derive from planetary influences, whilst astronomy deals with the material laws relating to those stars. The basis of the astrologer's studies and work centres around four chief categories – the sun, moon and other planets of our solar system (including the visual concourse of other stars), the zodiac, the houses of the horoscope and the planetary aspects. All the celestial bodies in our solar system emanate strong vibrations which react upon terrestrial life in various ways. The astrologer's work is thus concerned with the way in which these vibrations affect humanity, as a whole, or the individual being. His eventual assessments depend upon his ability as an astrologer, and can be tabled thus:

1 His astronomical and mathematical ability which will enable him to accurately estimate the positions of the planets of the Solar System at any specified moment in time.

2 His knowledge of planetary vibrations in order to assess their power and effect upon an individual or a whole nation.

3 His ability as an astrologer to decide how these vibrations may affect an individual or a nation.

The astrologer is interested in what predictions for the future can be obtained from these vibrations. However, this is not his sole preoccupation. He is also interested to see what effects the vibrations produce *now*, in order that he can compare and contrast his results with those achieved by astrologers of the past. As to the idea propagated that there is some element of mystery about the workings of astrology – the realities of trigonometrical and mathematical calculations engage his attention far too much for him to be bothered by anything else. Astrology, as with most other subjects, covers a number of subsidiary subjects which constitute the whole. We will be concerned mainly with natal astrology and, to a lesser degree, mundane astrology.

Natal Astrology.

Natal astrology relates to the birth of the individual. A natal astrological chart is erected, showing the actual positions of the sun, moon and other planets at the moment of the individual's birth. This chart is called a horoscope.

A horoscope for an individual's birth time is called a natus, nativity or a geniture. From the Natus, a series of psychological, physiological and other factors that are likely to affect his life can be deduced. Natal astrology is designated the most important branch of astrology as it relates to the individual.

Mundane Astrology

This branch of astrology deals with national and mundane matters. It is concerned with the effects of planetary influences on nations. As with natal astrology, a chart plotting the positions of the planets at a given moment in time is erected so that political, economic, agricultural, and other assessments that could affect a nation, can be deduced. Mundane astrology is bristling with technicalities which are of little consequence to the individual. Other divisions of the science include medical and agricultural astrology, and astro-suggestion which are of relatively little importance. The main emphasis though is centred on the socio-economic aspects of a nation.

The Solar System, and Table of Planets

What we call the universe is, in reality, a misnomer. The correct term for it is the Solar System. Our sun, together with its nine planets (six of which have one or more moons), constitute this solar or sun-system. The universe itself comprises a myriad other solar systems, some of which can be detected with the naked eye and others that are only faintly discernable with the most powerful of telescopic equipment. Where in the universe is humanity? Initially, we must pinpoint its position. Out of sheer misinformation, we consider the earth to be the centre of the solar system. This, of course, is a completely false impression. The sun is the nucleus of our solar system, and attached to it by centrifugal forces are the other nine planets and a belt of asteroids called Ceres. The planets follow fluc-

Below: *The Egyptian cosmos shown here is bounded by the sky goddess Nut, arching over the reclining god Queb who represents the earth, and enclosing magical symbols of Egyptian life.*

Below: *In this 17th century woodcut, parts of the body are linked to the sign of the zodiac with which they are associated.*

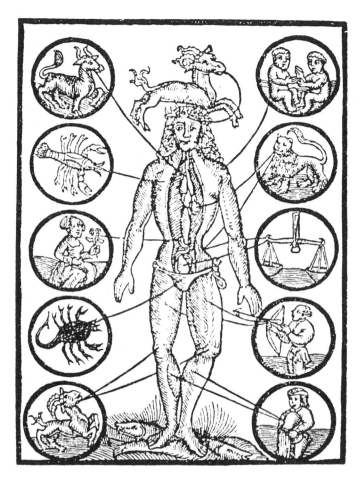

Above: *16th Century Astrologers casting a horoscope directly from the heavens at the moment of the birth of the child.*

tuating paths of orbit around the sun. We are the inhabitants of the planet Earth, a relatively small sphere, third in order of precedence from the sun, with only Mercury and Venus interposing. The earth covers incredible distances in its orbit of the sun – all a part of its work in some inexplicable master plan. To attempt to imagine the complete scheme, of which we are a part, would be futile and an impossibility, as our minds at this stage of evolution are incapable of absorbing and understanding the fact that we are but the tiniest particle of a micro-dot in a tiny solar system, tucked away in one corner of the universe. What that plan is, or who the formulator may be, is an unanswerable question and is essentially the whole basis of religion. To Christians, Moslems, Buddhists, Jews, or any other member of any other denomination one might care to name, God, even by his thousand other names, is the Master Planner, the formulator of all that is.

To the rest, who prefer to place their faith in astrology, rather than religious beliefs, there can be no peace of mind as in the sanctuary of religion. Astrology, still in an embryonic state even after 5,000 years, is an insoluble puzzle, a plague that has no cure. But to the chosen few, it is a superior science, wherein is contained the true answer to the age old questions of why we are here and who put us here. We, in the minority, are as close to the answer as we are to infinity – and forever is a long way off. Whatever the solution, the intelligence behind this master plan of ours (and there can be no plan without some intelligence to formulate it) is deserving of homage – if only because of the unique problem man has been set.

Table of Planets in Order of Sequence from the Sun

(All mean distances and speeds per hour in miles)

Planet	Symbol	Distance	Diameter	Speed	Moons
The Sun	Shield of the Sun God, Helios ⊙				
Mercury	The Cadeuceus (winged staff) of Hermes ☿	33.9 million	3,100	105,000	0
Venus	Circle surmounting a cross ♀	67.8 million	7,600	77,050	0
Earth	Circle with a cross ⊕	92.8 million	7,926	66,533	1
Mars	Shield of Ares, God of War, with an arrow glancing off it. ♂	141.5 million	4,200	53,090	2
Jupiter	First letter of the Greek word Zeus. ♃	484 million	88,700	28,744	9
Saturn	Sickle of Chronos, God of Time ♄	885 million	75,100	21,221	9
Uranus	Circle surmounted by letter H, after Herschel, the discoverer of the planet. ♅	1,782 million	30,900	14,960	4
Neptune	The Trident of Neptune, ruler of the sea. ♆	2,793 million	33,000	11,958	1
Pluto	A circle with a horizontal band. ♇	3,670 million	3,600	10,400	0

The Solar System and the Individual

From the chart of the table of planets, it can be seen that the distances of the planets from the sun are inconceivably great. However, it must be realised that the nearest fixed star (celestial bodies of other solar systems) that we can discern, is some seven thousand times further from the sun than Pluto is – a mere 25 billion miles. A fact about the solar system that should be noted is that as with some great machine that

Above: *"As above, so below", the underlying belief of astrology is expressed in this image of man, the microcosm overlaid on the universe, or macrocosm.*

depends upon the effectiveness and good working order of each individual part, a minor breakdown that may affect any one part of it could possibly affect the whole machine as a matter of consequence. Such is the case of the human body when illness affects it. The stomach or head might be affected and at times the body feels unable to cope satisfactorily with the extra work load imposed upon it – thus breaking down temporarily.

It has become increasingly evident that the solar system suffers and is elated in exactly the same manner as the body. This fact is of great importance as it now makes it possible for man to explore and maybe discover the root causes of the afflictions and pleasures that affect terrestrial life – if, as it is now generally accepted, everything works in accordance with this law. If, by the same reasoning, we can discover by what law the earth feels the reactions of the solar system, it may be possible to discover what motivates the actions of whole nations at times and, what is more important, what motivates the individual. Here we get to the very roots of astrology. Science accepts the fact that the condition of the solar system is reflected in the condition of the earth. Centuries ago, it was discovered that the state of the planets conditions every human being. Investigations have progressed for some 5,000 years to this end and history has preserved many detailed and documented proofs which have multiplied thousand-fold since the establishment of astrology as a science. So it can be seen that the sun, moon and planets comprise the main elements of our solar system. The sun is a star, just as are all the planets that revolve around it in their orbits, and six of the planets each have one or more satellites that in turn revolve around them in their orbits. The earth has one satellite, the moon, which is regarded as a planet for the sake of astrological convenience. The satellites of the other planets are of no apparent astrological significance.

The Twelve Groups of the Zodiac

The following is a list of the Twelve Groups, together with English and Latin names, and the limits of the 'traditional' zodiac. It must be remembered that the 'traditional' zodiac – called 'tropical' – used throughout the astrology world for many centuries, is out of step with the 'sidereal' zodiac. When traditional astrology says, for example, that the sun is in Aquarius, it is really in the preceding constellation, Capricorn, and so on right round the zodiac circle. Astrologers have begun to take notice of this fact since the turn of the century.

Astrological Sequence	Symbol	Traditional Limits
Aries	Ram	Mar 21 to Apr 19
Taurus	Bull	Apr 20 to May 20
Gemini	Twins	May 21 to Jun 20
Cancer	Crab	Jun 21 to Jul 20
Leo	Lion	Jul 21 to Aug 22
Virgo	Young Girl	Aug 23 to Sep 22
Libra	Scales	Sep 23 to Oct 22
Scorpio	Scorpion	Oct 23 to Nov 21
Sagittarius	Archer	Nov 22 to Dec21
Capricorn	Goat	Dec 22 to Jan 19
Aquarius	Water Carrier	Jan 20 to Feb 18
Pisces	Fish	Feb 19 to Mar 20

The Zodiac

The zodiac is an invisible belt that lies around the earth, indicating the orbit of the sun, the moon and the other planets. The outline of the zodiac can be seen when noting the positions of the planets at night. It is divided into 12 signs each of 30 degrees, making a total of 360° (the sum total of degrees in a cycle). Degrees can be divided into minutes and seconds. These symbols are appropriate when referring to celestial longitude, as opposed to the use of abbreviations m. and s. for minutes and seconds of time. The zodiac is constructed from seven cosmic principles, four of which are called the elements and the other three being called qualities. These principles give rise to this division of the zodiac into 12 groups. The Elements (also called Trigons or Triplicities), are symbolically named Fire, Air, Water and Earth, and the Qualities (also called Quadruplicities) or modes of action, are named Cardinal, Fixed or Mutable states. Four signs belong to each of the Qualities giving us the table below:

Qualities		
Cardinal	**Fixed**	**Mutable**
Aries	Leo	Sagittarius
Cancer	Scorpio	Pisces
Libra	Aquarius	Gemini
Capricorn	Taurus	Virgo

One of each group of the Cardinal, Fixed and Mutable Qualities, belongs to each of the Elements. Thus our final table of signs will appear as follows:

Qualities			
Elements	**Cardinal**	**Fixed**	**Mutable**
Fire	Aries	Leo	Sagittarius
Air	Libra	Aquarius	Gemini
Earth	Capricorn	Taurus	Virgo
Water	Cancer	Scorpio	Pisces

Further division of the elements can be made, into positive and negative groups. Fire and Air signs are known as positive groups, and Earth and Water signs are the negative groups. Positive groups are dominant, aggressive and generally extroverted types. Negative groups are

more feminine, inclined to be instinctively protective, and rely mainly on intuition.

Ruling Planets

Each sign (and sometimes two) is 'ruled' by one of the planets of the solar system. The sun, as the giver of life, rules a positive sign and the moon, as the sustainer of that life, rules a negative sign. For the rest, Mercury, Venus and Mars · rule two signs while Jupiter, Saturn, Uranus and Neptune rule one each. Pluto, the planet that indicates the beginning and ending of life,· has no definite rulership, though it has some connection with Scorpio. The term Exaltation is to be specially noted as it indicates a sign in which a planet, when present, is said to be favourable These 'exaltations' or favourable conditions occur when the sun is in Aries; Mercury is in Virgo; Mars is in Capricorn; Saturn is in Libra; the moon is in Taurus; Venus is in Pisces and Jupiter is in Cancer.

The Signs

The signs themselves commence at 0° of Aries (the first of the signs in sequence), which is the

Above: *Jupiter, the ruler of the heavens. On his chariot wheels are the symbols of Pisces and Sagittarius, the signs of which he is ruler, and to which he gives his qualities.*

point of the zodiac where the sun crosses the Equator (March 21st, the Vernal Equinox) in passing into North Declination and they extend around the circumference of the zodiac circle, at 30° intervals, ending at 30° of Pisces. (All astrological terms are defined on page 17.) The signs are seen to be of 30° each but this angle can have a further significant division into Decans. Decans are the division of a sign of 30° into three equal angles of 10° each.

We have already suggested that the zodiac can be imagined as an invisible belt that lies around the earth. Our next objective is to expand upon this and put the whole idea of the zodiac into proper perspective. In simplified terms, if we imagine the sky as a giant sphere, with the earth pin-pointed at the nucleus of this sphere, it would appear that the sun and planets orbit the earth over a period of one year. This path taken by the sun is called the Ecliptic and its plane is inclined between 23° and 27° from that of the Celestial Equator. The point where the Ecliptic cuts the Celestial Equator is called point Gamma (♈). It must also be remembered that the plane of the Ecliptic is not perpendicular to the line of the poles, around which the earth rotates on its axis. This motion is, as we already know, only apparent, but it must be remembered that astrologers' interests centre around apparent motions. The planets follow the same course as the sun in their orbit, within the confines of an invisible 'belt', which extends no further than 8° either side of the Ecliptic.

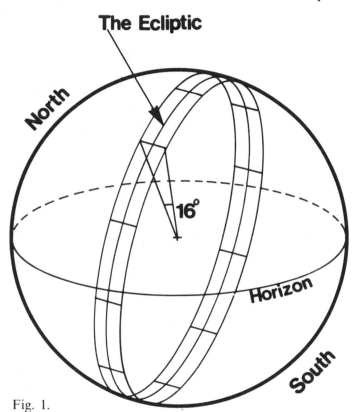

Fig. 1.
The Ecliptic, with the belt of the Zodiac extending 8° either side.

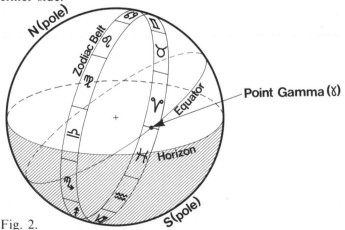

Fig. 2.
Diagram showing where the plane of the Ecliptic cuts the Celestial Equator (Point Gamma ♈)

The Twelve Houses

Whereas the zodiac is made up of 12 sections, each one of 30°, the houses of the horoscope, too, are divided into 12 parts, but they do not necessarily contain angular values of 30° each as they are variable in value. The houses and the zodiac are not coincidental either. We must realise that the zodiac is part of the sky itself, whilst the houses are fixed. As the earth spins on its axis, the sky moves from east to west, once every 24 hours, whilst the planets in reality move in their orbit around the sun, from west to east through the signs of the zodiac. Because of this rotation, all the stars appear to travel across the Celestial Sphere in the course of a day. Astrology, therefore, treats each one-day cycle as a miniature year.

The houses of the horoscope have no names as such, but are numbered in automatic sequence from the 1st to the 12th House, in a reverse direction from the Diurnal Motion of the planets, beginning at the Ascendant. Astrologers attach great importance to the Ascendant. In setting up a Natus, the sign in which the Ascendant appears is as important as the sign in which the sun appears, for the influences of both signs if mixed. At this stage the preceding passage may well tend to confuse the reader, but suffice to say that it will become much clearer as we proceed. As we have stated, the houses are the resultant divisions of the Diurnal Motion of the stars and, as such, are fixed. The diagram illustrates this adequately.

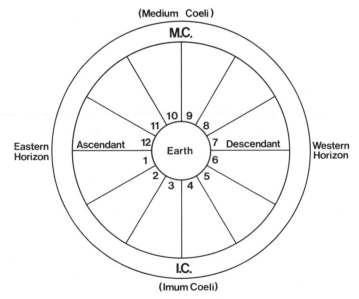

Diagram showing the houses in relation to the Western and Eastern Horizons and the Midheaven (M.C.)

The above houses, which correspond to the Cardinal signs, Aries, Cancer, Libra and Capricorn, are termed Angular. A planet is considered 'strong or dominant' in an Angular House. The houses corresponding to the Fixed signs (2nd, 5th, 8th, 11th) are termed Succedent. A planet is 'moderately strong' when in a succedent house.

The houses corresponding to the Mutable signs (3rd, 6th, 9th, 12th) arc termcd Cadcnt. A planet is 'weak' when placed in a Cadent house.

Astrological Terms

Horoscope: a diagram showing the geocentric positions of the Sun, Moon and planets. All planetary positions are calculated in relation to a given moment of time and specific geographical latitude and longitude. A horoscope erected upon the basis of a known birth time and geographical co-ordinate contains the following factors: zodiacal sectors; planets in their respective zodiacal positions; 12 houses, the boundary of the first being the ascendent; fair angles or planetary aspects.

Sign: sector of the zodiac through which the sun was passing at the moment N. was born.

Zodiac: a notional band of sky representing the Sun's annual path through the fixed stars. It consists of twelve sectors measuring 30 degrees each. The sectors are named after fixed constellations: Aries, Taurus, etc.

Ephemeris (pl. Ephemerides): table containing the daily noon positions of Sun, Moon and planets.

Ascendant: position on a horoscope of the rising Sun.

Medium Coeli: position on a horoscope of the Sun at noon.

Descendant: position on a horoscope of the Sun at evening.

Immum Coelis: position on a horoscope of the Sun at midnight.

Angles: Axes on a horoscope of the Ascendant/Descendant and the MC/IC.

Sidereal Time: Time told according to star positions, not the clock.

House: Division of the horoscope numbered anti-clockwise from the Ascendant.

Cusp: Boundary of a house.

Aspects: Certain angular distances, expressed in degrees, between any two or more planets. Most important are:

Conjunction	0°
Square	90°
Trine	120°
Sesqui-quadrate	145°
Opposition	180°
Semi-square	45°
Sextile	60°

Aspects: *Conjunction* (0°) or *opposition* (180°) can be either good or bad, according to the planets concerned.

Square (90°) and *semi-square* (45°) are malefic; *trine* (120°) and *sextile* (60°) are beneficient.

Dominant Planets: Those close to MC and the Ascendant.

Celestial: The term used to distinguish from geographical.

Celestial Equator: The continued projection of the equator to the heavens.

Celestial Sphere: The sky, when assumed to be a great sphere, with the Earth pinpointed at the centre of it.

Ecliptic: The Ecliptic is a great circle of the celestial sphere through which the sun traces a course in one year at the rate of about 1° per day.

Diurnal Motion: A complete revolution of the Earth on its Polar Axis through a 24 hour period.

Celestial Latitude: The distance of a body North or South from the Ecliptic.

Celestial Longitude: The distance of a body from 0° Aries (the start of the Zodiac). For example, we would say a body is in 1° of Taurus, meaning that it is placed one sign away from 0° of Aries.

Right Ascension: Measured along the Equator from 0° Aries.

Declination: Measured North or South of the Equator.

*Seasonal activities on earth and in the Zodiac
in these pages from the* Tres Riches Heures *of the
Duc du Berri.* **Below:** *September; harvesters in
the fields while Virgo and Libra are dominant.*

Giraudon

Below left: *October; the workers are preparing the fields for spring and Libra gives place to Scorpio*
Below right: *December; the excitement of the boar hunt; in the sky, Sagittarius and Capricorn.*

The Planets

The rays of the sun produce the energy to give and maintain the element of life. The moon, which does not produce any energy or light of its own, throws off the sun's reflected rays, which affect many people on the earth when the moon is in its various phases. The same can be said of the other planets with regard to the fact that the vibrations emanated by them affect individual beings on earth in various ways in varying degrees of influence. Thousands of years ago, astrologers discovered that when the planets were in a certain state and moved into certain positions, the chain of human events was affected in various ways, taking definite shape – as though our destiny really was written in the stars. It has also been recorded that when the conditions of these planetary states are duplicated, then so too are the conditions on earth duplicated. As with precise science, astrologers have made their own calculations and the results are proof enough of the extent of planetary influence. We can therefore deduce that the planets exercise a definite influence on every terrestrial being, which influence affects our environment. We may also deduce that these influences which the planets exercise are natural to them and are also exclusive to them.

There is never the slightest doubt as to which planet is exercising its influence and when the intricacies of astrological mathematics have been mastered, it will be comparatively easy to state just when the individual planet is exerting force on the earth's conditions. We can now touch upon the question of the characteristics of each of the planets and also the strength of their actions, so that we might analyse the purpose each planet plays with regard to the "Master Plan" of the universe. Every horoscope contains the sun, moon and eight other planets, and the influences of them affect the lives of every individual to some extent or other. It must be realised, though, that the Natus (chart) of each individual varies in this respect. The strength of the planets depends upon the position of the signs, the position of the houses and the aspects contained in the horoscope. Whether the action of a planet will be harmonious and beneficial or retarding and discordant, depends upon the zodiac and aspect strength. A planet will obviously be strongest in the sign(s) it rules, but it will also be very strong in its exaltation. Thus, although Venus in Libra produces a "don't bring me into it" characteristic, in its exaltation, Pisces, the character tends to become more benign and sympathetic to the less fortunate. Let us now consider the character and work of each planet in chronological sequence, commencing with the sign(s) ruled by each planet, an indication of the Quality and Element, the Exaltation (if any) and the planets' nature of action – benefic, malefic or neutral. *Benefics,* if well placed, are conducive to good luck and easy success without much difficulty. If badly placed, they indicate the less serious misfortunes that may befall the individual. *Malefics,* if well placed, will indicate success can be achieved by the subject through sheer hard work and a concerted effort to succeed. If badly placed, they show exceptionally bad conditions for the subject and could possibly degenerate to a rather dangerous disposition. The action of *Neutrals* is determined in accordance with their positioning in the horoscope.

Characteristics and Work

The Sun

Sign: Leo – Fixed Fire
Exaltation: Aries
Nature of Action: Neutral

The sun is the giver of life. It produces the energy that endows animals and plants with that life. It stimulates the positive power in our nature, urging us forward to greater heights. Physical strength and vigour are ever present. The vibrations of the sun produce a sense of dignity, a will to construct and build, a strong character and keen appreciation. It creates an affectionate and self-reliant person, who is big hearted, magnanimous and effervescent. If the sun is placed badly in the horoscope, these qualities will not be present. The character will tend to be pretentious, often saying he is going to do something but seldom getting around to doing it or, at least, actually achieving very little. He tries to lead but is, in fact, the one that is led. Superficial affection will hide excessive selfishness, and such people are incompetent and egocentric to a fault. The sun's influence is particularly striking in people who constitute the government of society, monarchs, popes, emperors and all political leaders. In lesser spheres, the sun indicates the father's personality, or a husband's personality in a wife's chart. The sun (and moon) is called a Light (or

Luminary). The sun has special care for the most vital parts of the body such as head, heart, back, eyes, spermatazoa and blood circulation. Attention to physical growth and the flow of vital forces is his special domain.

Mercury

Signs: Gemini – Mutable Air
     Virgo – Mutable Earth
Exaltation: Virgo
Nature of Action: Neutral

The planet Mercury represents the mind, reasoning, logic, speech and writing. Thus it is known as the planet of the intellect. Wherever speedy thought processes are brought into action, Mercury dominates. It rules all aspects of literature, writings, thoughts and ideas. It also rules trade, commerce and travel (especially short distances). In business, the position of the planet is invaluable. Subjects whose ruling planet is Mercury are often good talkers, but do not have a great deal of imagination. If badly placed, there may be a tendency to bad temper, deviousness, petty arguing and quarreling, exaggeration and an inclination to 'live by one's wits', rather than a more specifically stable application of the mental dexterity of the character. Lying, sarcasm, and general instability may be significant traits. Mercury controls the general nerve and respiratory systems, the tongue, the senses, the spinal nervous system and the intestines. Diseases that may be attributable to the planet are bad nerves, epileptic diseases and neurasthenia.

Venus

Signs: Libra – Cardinal Air
     Taurus – Fixed Earth
Exaltation: Pisces
Nature of Action: Lesser Benefic

Venus symbolises the emotions of love, beauty and harmony. Venus is the loved rather than the lover. It is understanding, appreciative of beauty in every conceivable shape or form, and shapes the influence of physical contact with others. All that is refined, elegant, sympathetic and fashionable is dominated by Venus. When well placed, Venusians are unbiased, refined, agreeable, artistic, devoted to pursuing social pleasures and delights, amiable and often unused to hard work. When afflicted, it can lead to sheer laziness, total reliance upon other people, slackness, impracticality, dreaminess and

sometimes lack of confidence. In the body Venus regulates the kidneys, reproductive system, mouth and throat. Diseases that may be attributable to the planet are kidney diseases such as nephritis.

The Moon

Signs: Cancer – Cardinal Water
Exaltation: Taurus
Nature of Action: Neutral

As the sun gives life, so the moon maintains and protects that life. The moon has no light of its own, but reflects the rays of the sun which affect many individuals on earth. The moon's work, as we have learned over many centuries, is to care for the emotional side of our life. It stimulates the maternal and protective instincts within us. As the sun represents fire, so the moon has domain over water. The tides rise and fall with the waxing and waning of the moon. The moon influences all that is feminine, passive and prudent. In the horoscope, the moon indicates the woman's personality. In the chart of a man, it indicates the influence of a woman over the subject. The emotions are affected by the changing phases of the moon. Depression, elation, happiness and sadness all fluctuate as the moon passes from one stage into another. As the sun indicates the positive, outgoing side of the individual, with the ability to express himself, so the moon indicates the more introverted, receptive and intuitive side of the individual. These beings tend to be careful, very meek and timid, and often lead sheltered lives. Given to moods, they are changeable, fickle, highly emotional and very patient. People with psychic power have strong moon influences and artists have strongly aspected moons. The lunar character can be ultra-sensitive and self-conscious, narrow minded and tends to be prejudicial in discriminatory processes. The moon presides over the physical body and its work centres around the stomach, mucous membranes and the nutritive systems.

Mars

Signs: Aries – Cardinal Fire
     Scorpio – Fixed Water
     (Jointly with Pluto)
Exaltation: Capricorn
Nature of Action: Lesser Malefic

Mars is the energising planet. It rules the power of will and the impulses that result in activity and violent or turbulent movement. Whereas the sun gives life and the moon maintains that life, the function of Mars, which is less stable than the sun and moon, is to energise and vitalise living matter and to induce activity, enterprise, endurance, great courage and nerve. Mars stimulates restlessness, recklessness and egocentricity. There is a complete lack of finesse when dealing with people, a tendency not to mince words but to get straight down to business. Quarrelsome and bigoted, the Mars subject believes he can do things for himself better than with help from others. When badly placed, it can result in extreme brutality and cruel treatment of others and ruthlessness when wanting to get on with things. The subject can be extremely impolite, preferring to dispense with courtesies. Martian subjects have a great desire for freedom and liberty, which can make them heroic champions of the less fortunate. Mars has control over muscular tissue, nose, motor nervous system, generative organs and red corpuscles, and also the skull and face, and the excretory system. Diseases attributable to the planet are complaints of pain due to stress, strain and overwork, all fever complaints and inflammatory diseases.

Jupiter
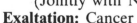

Signs: Sagittarius — Mutable Fire
　　　Pisces — Mutable Water
　　　(Jointly with Neptune)
Exaltation: Cancer
Nature of Action: Greater Benefic
Jupiter is concerned with the fortunes and good luck of the individual, especially where expansion is occurring. The more generous impulses such as foresight, logic and humanitarianism are ever present. It is the universal symbol of authority. Its domains include knowledge, science and sportsmanship. The action is of a mental nature and indicates kindliness, loyalty, generosity and optimism. Jupiter subjects are blessed with more than the average amount of good luck although not necessarily because they deserve it. If badly placed, the planet makes for an excessive use of energy, over-indulgence and an over-optimistic attitude. The character will tend to rely on his luck unnecessarily, taking unreasonable risks and gambles. Jupiter is concerned with the blood, the liver, building organisms and the flesh, and also rules nutrition.

Saturn
ħ

Signs: Aquarius — Fixed Air
　　　(Jointly with Uranus)
　　　　Capricorn — Cardinal Earth
Exaltation: Libra
Nature of Action: Greater Malefic
Saturn is the planet of strict justice and has authority over the safeguarding of human life. The conservative, practical planet, it influences the material element of life. When the planet is well placed, the individual is self-sustaining, with virtues such as thriftiness, industriousness, endurance, reliability, stability, patience and good concentration. But there are also limitations on the individual's views and sympathies, making him cautious and narrow-minded. If badly placed, it indicates selfishness, a miserly attitude to others and a lack of foresight or optimism. The Saturnian believes that everything is gained through hard work and not through luck or good fortune. The planet represents all that is old, inflexible and traditional, and symbolises materialism and true worth, endowing all things with their lasting and permanent qualities. It also symbolises trials and tribulations, barriers, bad luck, and a slowly consuming enmity, that could very well smoulder for many years. It is the planet of misfortune, reflecting greed, avarice, extreme oppression, hatred and poverty. It is also a planet of retarding effects, causing delays and disappointments and setting limits on individual efforts. Saturn rules the skin and bones, in particular the cartilages and tendons, also the general skeletal structure, including articulation of the bones and the accumulative processes of the body. Diseases attributable to the planet are chronic illnesses, usually the result of poor living and severe hardship, and also melancholia, hereditary diseases and rheumatism.

Uranus (Also called Herschel)
⛢

Signs: Aquarius — Fixed Air
　　　(Joint ruler with Saturn)
Nature of Action: Malefic
Uranus symbolises inventive powers, upheaval, change and tension. It also rules flexibility, originality, intellect, patience, common sense

Right: *August from the* Tres Riches Heures.
The chariot of the sun, shining on the gleaners below, seen as journeying through the circle of the zodiac.

and leadership. It tends to produce unconventional and revolutionary people, not aggressively so, but in a genial, outspoken, forthright way. Uranus reflects a combination of traits, common to the sun, Mercury, Mars and Saturn. When badly placed it inclines to produce eccentricity. It typifies the genius who is always wasting his time on frivolous, self-indulgent schemes, common sense seldom prevailing in his fight against convention. The subject may also display extreme bad temper, over-sensitivity and a bitter disposition towards those he feels have slighted or insulted him. Bouts of severe moodiness, affecting all who comes into contact with the subject, may be significantly prominent. Although the influence of Uranus, at its best, may endow the individual with a fine, original mind, at its worst the character may be unsavoury, highly undependable and even possibly a little unbalanced. The physical rulership of Uranus is the nervous system, and one of the diseases attributable to the planet is paralysis.

Neptune

Sign: Pisces — Mutable Water
(Joint Ruler with Jupiter)

Nature of Action: Malefic

Neptune symbolises the mind on the higher plane: spiritualism, psychism and mysticism. It can also induce a chaotic state. As Uranus reflects characteristics of the sun, Mars, Saturn and Mercury, so Neptune reflects Venus and Jupiter. It symbolises the creative imagination, fantasy (as in films and theatre) and the intuitive mind. It can also produce pretentiousness, falsehood, deception, dishonesty in spiritual and material matters, a state of chaos, discord, the use of poisons and drugs which induce hallucinatory effects (this too, is a characteristic of Jupiter), espionage, both military and industrial, and unconstructive idealism. When the planet is badly placed, if care and common sense is not exercised, the individual can find himself in dreadful predicaments, causing great distress, and his disposition may jeopardise the well-being of others. Neptune can be ideally referred to as utopianism that has wandered into an anarchistic, chaotic world. The planet, like Uranus, has charge of the nervous system. Diseases attributable to it are extreme physical sensitivity, hallucinations, delusions, morbid fears, acute nervous stress ailments, and severe anxiety.

Pluto

Sign: Undetermined but an
affinity with Scorpio
(Jointly ruled with Mars) — Fixed Water

Nature of Action: Malefic

Pluto rules catastrophes and great disasters, sudden upheavals such as earthquakes and volcanic eruptions preceding more stable conditions; death, agony, clairvoyance, the occult, spiritualism. It is symbolic of the cult of Nazism and the Atomic Bomb and it is called the planet of the 'healing crisis'. It also presides over the shadows, the invisible side of things, the unknown. Lying on the edge of the solar system, Pluto is the guardian of the infinite. It indicates the start and the finish of life.

Sun and moon, undergoing transmutation.

The Qualities and Elements

	Positive		Negative	
	Fire	Air	Earth	Water
Cardinal	Mars	Venus	Saturn	Moon
Fixed	Sun	Saturn (Uranus)	Venus	Mars (Pluto)
Mutable	Jupiter	Mercury	Mercury	Jupiter (Neptune)

The table of Qualities and Elements is now shown with the ruling planets inserted (including joint rulers, Pluto, Uranus, and Neptune) for the actual signs. From the table it can be seen that Mercury and Jupiter each rule two Mutable signs and no other qualities can be stated to be Mutable in their nature of action. The sun rules one Fixed Fire sign and the moon rules one Cardinal Water sign. Mars, Venus and Saturn rule one Cardinal and one Fixed sign each. Uranus has an affinity with the Fixed Air side of

Saturn, Pluto an affinity with the Fixed Water side of Mars, and Neptune with the Mutable Water side of Jupiter.

The Qualities

The Qualities (also called Quadruplicities because they each consist of four signs) comprise three groups of four signs each.

Cardinal Signs

The cardinal signs are the activity signs. They are energetic, enterprising, boisterous and outgoing types. When afflicted, the Cardinal signs show restlessness and instability. Indolence and lack of imagination are strikingly prominent.

Fixed Signs

The Fixed signs influence feeling, intuition, sense and "pleasure-pain" aspects. They are relatively stable and conservative, and stubborn in the sense that they hold fixed opinions. When afflicted, they become exceptionally lazy, over-indulgent, self-centred, unprincipled, inconsistent and immune to reason.

Mutable Signs

These signs fluctuate between the Cardinal and Fixed signs. They indicate the mental processes of the subject. Their attitude is to try and understand all things. They are intelligent, clever, versatile, flexible and changeable and are blessed with great mental dexterity. When afflicted, they become capricious and unstable, disloyal to those who depend on them, unimaginative, flippant and irreverent. They may incline to egoism, extreme selfishness and a notable inability to make decisions. The Mutable signs are sometimes referred to as 'common signs' because they have something of both the Cardinal and Fixed qualities in them. Whether or not a Quality (or Element) is strong or weak, is dependant upon how many planets are contained in the Cardinal, Fixed or Mutable signs. We must also consider the Ascendant and the fact that a strongly placed planet can sustain any lack of quality.

The Elements
Fire

This is the element of activity, push, and strong self-assertion. It is positive, loyal, hopeful, aggressive, self-assured and powerful. Fiery subjects are inclined to like all sport, a high standard of living and enjoy good company. They are the pioneering types and seekers of new thrills and new adventures – regardless of the risks they might entail. The faults are excessive exuberance and extravagance, over-optimism, egoism, arrogance, brashness, a lack of sympathy for the less fortunate and too much pride. When the element is lacking, the subject becomes boorish. His spirits are dampened and he lacks an enthusiastic approach to life.

Water

Water is opposite in nature to the Fire signs, indicating an introverted, instinctively protective, passively inclined person. Without water, fire would cause life to extinguish itself through exuberance, over-excess of energy and hastiness. Water signs have great vision and prudent qualities, maternal and protective instincts and they cultivate a great deal of sympathy. Their faults stem from being too afraid, introverted, suspicious and an inability to express themselves. Whilst Water signs are sensitive and introverted, keeping their feeling and thoughts to themselves, the Fire signs tends to be more extroverted and capable of self-expression. Both the Fire and Water signs are basic, relying more on instinct and spontaneity than on logical planning of schemes or projects.

Air

Air provides intelligent, logical, refined, highly developed thought processes and splendid reasoning powers. The virtues of the Air signs lie in the constant need for truth. It is intellectual, unbiased, harmonious and co-operative. Its faults stem from instability, capriciousness, dreaminess, an inability to divorce reality from fantasy, lack of concentration, bad decision making and an ability but not the energy to get down to necessary tasks.

Earth

Earth signs indicate concrete or practical values, patience, hard-work, concentration, reliability, and sensible material values. Whereas Air signs are the planners or designers, so Earth signs execute the actual construction of the plan. Their faults may be narrow-mindedness, materialism, selfishness, sordidness, and an inability to produce good results. They can be rather boring and mundane in their approach to life.

Below: *March Spring planting influenced by Pisces and Aries. More pages from* Tres Riches Heures *again linking heaven and earth in seasonal appropriateness.*

Below left: *April is the month of spring courtship and spring flowers of Aries and Taurus.* **Right:** *A flower decked procession setting out to honour the first of May.*

Characteristics of the Signs of the Zodiac

The signs of the zodiac bestow characteristics and qualities, both good and bad, upon the subjects born under them. Our main objective is to see how each of the groups reacts physically, mentally and emotionally, taking into account the fact that there are interacting influences that may affect the individual. When we have learned the characteristics of the signs, and have taken into account the position of the planets which may occupy our own sign or, in the case of ascending signs, have considered the position of the ruling planet by house, sign and aspect, we may be able to draw positive conclusions that may help us in everyday life. We will then be in a position to compare ourselves as we actually are and as we really should be according to the laws of astrology. This could be a decisive factor in stimulating the subject into remedying the defects which would appear to be non-characteristic of a particular sign, or may be faults of that sign. One should remember that for the sake of accuracy, a horoscope for each individual should be set up, otherwise we can only speak in very general terms. Another interesting feature is the matter of correspondences. Every sign contains a related world of colours, plants, animals, gemstones and occupations, which add to its sense of identity. To learn and know these correspondences adds to your self-awareness, from them you gain a wealth of understanding, sometimes mysterious and symbolic, sometimes direct and down to earth, but always enlightening.

THE SUN SIGNS

ARIES

♈

Aries, the Ram, first sign of the Zodiac
March 21st - April 20th
New beginnings, energy, leadership

Aries (Positive sign of Mars, Cardinal-Fire)

Compatible Signs: Leo and Sagittarius

Advantages of the Group

Arians demonstrate extreme physical courage and enthusiasm for all ideas. They possess unlimited energy in the handling of their affairs and are adventurous, bold and audacious in attacking problems at hand. Enterprising and capable of grasping opportunities they show great independence, mental dexterity in debate, and a general air of vigour which should be sensibly channelled. They are the world's great optimists, sincere in dealing with others and have a tendency to champion causes on behalf of the less fortunate.

Disadvantages of the Group

Bad types can be reckless and pig-headed, often involving the taking of unnecessary risks and indulging in foolhardy heroics. They are impulsive, quarrelsome, uncompromising and are wasteful with regard to physical and mental vigour. They can also be very impatient with slower people. The group has a tendency to act without first thinking of the consequences, usually with complete disregard for other people's feelings or rights. They are uncompromising, very easily provoked, aggressive, sarcastic, greedy, desirous of power, egocentric, imprudent, boastful, and their pride derives from stubbornness. There is a distinct lack of impartiality and because he never looks before he leaps, the Arian tends to 'step on' people in

Top: *Baudelaire, whose adventurous poetry is typical of his Aries sun sign.* **Left:** *Aries is associated with the eyes, this jewelled eye is by Salvador Dali.* **Above:** *A steelworker.*

his desire for power or promotion – thus gaining a reputation for ruthlessness.

Health Difficulties of the Group

Health difficulties are those associated with the head, brain, face, eyes, upper jaw, cerebrum and carotid arteries. Typical Aries diseases are brain fever, headaches, neuralgic and eye troubles, facial complaints such as toothache and gum-boils, and feverish sicknesses such as influenza. These are the main illnesses which should be avoided or safeguarded against. Headwounds, too, are a common occurrence amongst Arians.

Physical Appearance of the Group

The sign gives an energetic demeanour with a quick, darting appearance, rather a lean and wiry torso, and a long, slender neck. Its subjects are often round headed and snub-nosed, with a prominent chin. The teeth are quite prominent, the eyes usually hazel or grey, and the hair is reddish or light brown, usually curly or wiry.

Below: *The associations with fire and vigour make steelworking a typical Arian occupation.*
Overleaf: *Arian warriors in a stained glass.*

The Most Suitable Occupations

Military and associated professions are all suitable for this sign, and they also make good sportsmen, travellers, leaders and explorers. Any adventurous occupation is particularly agreeable to Arians. All branches of engineering and mechanical work attract them, also any profession utilising sharp instruments, such as doctors, surgeons and machinists. Retail buying and selling trades. The police force, fire service and any work where the use of metals or control of fire is necessary.

The Ideal for Success

The mind is of the executive type, confident, independent, ingenious and aggressive. Unfortunately the Arian tendency is to become far too ruthless and to excessively strain physical and emotional resources. The ideal for the sign is to keep a firm grip and to prevent unnecessary waste of energy and vigour. Learn to hold one's temper and avoid going to extremes. Also learn to reflect, and think deeply about all matters. Ambition should not be allowed to degenerate into greed and a lust for power, and a greater measure of genuine self-confidence sought.

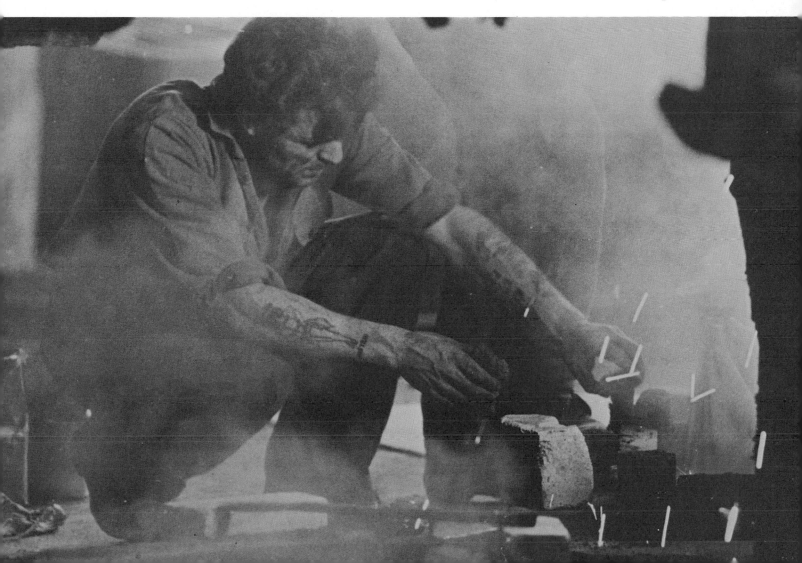

TAURUS

☿

Taurus, the Bull, second sign of the Zodiac
April 21st - May 21st
Steadfast, courageous, firm

Taurus (Negative of Venus, Fixed-Earth)

Compatible Signs: Virgo and Capricorn

Advantages of the Group

This group could be said to be the complete opposite of Aries and relates to the Venus type as far as refinement, culture, love of beauty and sensitivity are concerned. They show steadiness of character, patience, are practical, simple-natured, reserved, very kindly and completely honest. They show perseverance which allows them to overcome any obstacles, are protective, and enjoy simple pleasures. Taurus subjects demonstrate a degree of loyalty unsurpassed by any other group, are determined and even-tempered. In business they attain a great deal through sheer concentration, their dealings with others are honourable and they have good administrative ability (especially in money matters). Imperturbable, they love method and have an ordered, stable mind. They are a colourful, charming group, harmonious, fond of good food, music and painting and usually have good singing and speaking voices. The sign in fact produces many excellent singers.

Below: *Taureans enjoy both watching and joining in dancing.* **Below right:** *Sigmund Freud, the great psychoanalyst; he used his Taurean qualities to break through to a new understanding.*

Disadvantages of the Group

If badly placed, Taureans attach too great a significance to conservative ideas, with a consequent lack of flair and imagination. There is a tendency to boorishness and an inclination to become a stick-in-the-mud. A love of ease and an over-indulgence in food turns them into gluttons. There is a distinct lack of reasoning power and obstinacy manifests itself, where ordinary common sense ought to prevail. Procrastination and indolence due to their slowness in work, selfishness, avarice and meanness in financial dealings are all faults of the sign, and they can be reactionary, and untrustworthy. Once they have made up their minds about something, they are immovable, and this turns, at times, into fanaticism. They show jealousy of the success of others, lethargy and a refusal to make any effort to achieve goals. They become slovenly in attitude and completely lacking in vision or foresight.

Health Difficulties of the Group

In Taureans the parts of the body concerned with sickness and bad health are the neck, throat, ears, sense of taste, thyroid gland, lower jaw, tonsils, carotid arteries, jugular vein, larynx, pharynx and the back of the head. They are prone to throat infections, obesity, goitre, laryngitis, tonsillitis, croup, quinsy and diptheria.

Physical Appearance of the Group

They are solidly built but inclining to stoutness. A bull-like thick neck, powerful shoulders and rounded head are often typical, with blue or brown eyes, brown hair, usually dark and wavy, straight teeth and generally a ruddy complexion. Their manner is ponderous and their gait slow and deliberate.

The Most Suitable Occupations

Taureans excel in general constructional or building work, especially in executive positions. They can also prosper in most aspects of agriculture, such as farming and animal husbandry. Professions connected with fashion or jewellery, painting and decorating are also suitable. Many are found in work concerning a critical attitude towards food such as food inspectors, gourmets, etc. Artistic interests such as music (especially singing), poetry and painting

Top left: *A banquet; Taurus is usually a good cook.* **Bottom:** *The mouth is associated with the sign.* **Above:** *Taureans find satisfaction in farming, being an earth sign.*

are good outlets for the sign if a suitable profession can be found.

The Ideal for Success

The mind is thorough and constructive, rather than critical, and Taureans often have an unusually good memory. The character is steadfast, persistent and well-motivated, when at its best. Efforts should be made to keep a more open mind and to be less selfish and avaricious when the sign is badly placed. Efforts must also be made to cut out any excess of drinking and gluttony which may lead to obesity. Obstinacy, self-righteousness and lack of personal integrity also need to be overcome.

Venus, the ruler of Taurus, painted by Bronzino, 1503-72

❧ GEMINI ❧

Ⅱ

Gemini, the Twins, third sign of the Zodiac
May 22nd - June 21st
Duality, versatility, the intellect

Gemini (Positive of Mercury, Mutable-Air)

Compatible Signs: Libra and Aquarius

Advantages of the Group

Gemini is the sign of extreme mental dexterity, reason and logic, quickness and perception and speedy thought processes. Gemini subjects are ingenious, resourceful, versatile, intelligent, clever, generous, charming, vivacious, have good manners and are extremely adaptable. They excel above all other groups in their ability to grasp and understand facts and figures clearly and logically, prefer to rationalise without bias, and have a keen sense of appreciation, especially with regard to literature and art. The subjects are bright and vivacious conversationalists and debaters, and you should beware of getting your facts distorted otherwise the Gemini is liable to 'tear you to pieces'.

Disadvantages of the Group

The speed of their thought processes leads to superficiality, leaving problems either unfinished or with inconclusive answers. They tend to become unstable due to the inability to make decisions or make up their minds. Capriciousness, insufficient tact, lack of concentration, dishonesty when their cleverness enables them to 'live by their wits' are all faults of the sign and they often start many projects but frequently leave most or all of them unfinished, due to an extreme lack of concentration. There is a tendency to deceit and untruthfulness, over-extravagance, disloyalty and boorishness, egoism and pure selfishness.

Physical Appearance of the Group

They are generally of a fairly light build, but taller than average, and very straight-backed. Quick, darting eyes are common, usually brown or hazel, they are thin-lipped with aquiline noses, broad shouldered and flat chested. Their hair is usually straight and dark brown or black. The general appearance would indicate intelligence and acquisitiveness.

Health Difficulties of the Group

Health difficulties in Gemini afflict the arms, hands, shoulders, muscles, lungs and bones. Also the nerves, senses and vocal chords. Bronchial trouble, common colds and tuber-

Above top: A radio telescope, an image of Gemini receptivity. **Above:** *An unusual combination of Gemini characteristics made Queen Victoria a puzzling, enigmatic person.*

culosis are also prominent illnesses among Geminians, as are pleurisy, neuresthenia, asthma and nervous disorders. The group does appear to be able to overcome illnesses quite quickly, however.

The Most Suitable Occupations

Gemini subjects are most content with professions entailing writing or verbal expression. Journalists, authors, linguists, translators, secretaries, clerks, teachers are all occupations suitable for them as are all professions that disseminate knowledge. They are often connected with accountancy, high-powered salesmanship, travel, and make good interpreters.

Below: *Mercury, the quicksilver messenger of the Gods and ruling Planet of Gemini.* **Below right:** *Gemini subjects can be brilliant academics.*

The Ideal for Success

It could be said that the Gemini mind is brilliant – but in accordance with the standard of education. They are highly inventive subjects, very versatile and adaptable. When well educated, the mind is analytical and highly critical, but if not well educated, the Gemini may be criminally orientated or at the least, artful. The ability to think fast gives an air of great intellect, even though this may be purely superficial. Frequently this leads the Gemini subject to attempt to do too many things at once, and he may be constantly changing his job to suit his mental dexterity. Only when this diffuse tendency is overcome, when stability and greater concentration are achieved and when restlessness and nervousness are suitably controlled, can the subject reap the rewards of the sign's high intellectual power.

Left: *Birds are traditionally associated with Gemini.*
Below: *The image of The Twins, symbol of Gemini, is also supposed to indicate the conflict within the Gemini. Detail from Assyrian wall painting.*

CANCER

Cancer, the Crab, fourth sign of the Zodiac
June 22nd - July 23rd
Sensitive, maternal, very romantic

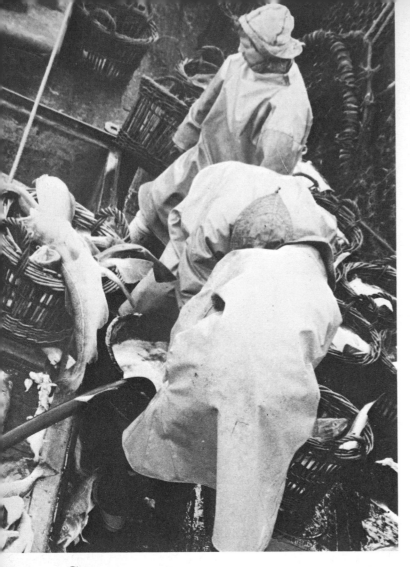

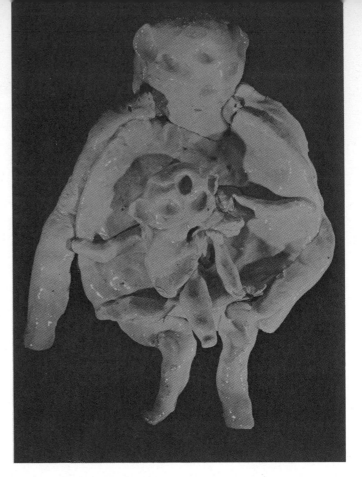

Left: *The element of water in Cancer encourages its subjects to seek maritime professions.* **Above:** *Cancer's association with motherhood and the womb is well expressed in this model by a child.*

Cancer (Negative Moon, Cardinal-Water)

Compatible signs: Pisces and Scorpio

Advantages of the Group

Cancer subjects reflect a sympathetic and humanitarian disposition but retain a discriminatory and judicial attitude. Extreme loyalty towards friends and devotion and faithfulness to any just and deserving cause are attributes of the sign. There is a marked preference for established order and the Cancer subjects do not often desire change. They have extreme physical and mental sensitivity, but in steadier types, there is usually adequate control of the feelings. They tend to be sentimental, strongly devoted to the home and family, patriotic, kind, intuitive, tolerant and modest. Also they are imaginative, serene, romantic and persistent. In their business activities, self-reliance, love of method, shrewdness and thrift are strongly reflected. They are endowed with a kindly sense of humour, great tenacity and perseverance and strong protective instincts.

The Disadvantages of the Group

Cancer subjects become unstable and unreliable at times. Sheer vanity creeps into the personality, eventually leading to frivolity and pride. Morbidity, procrastination, timidity and moodiness are all traits of the bad Cancer subject. They can become over-sensitive which gives them inferiority complexes, over-confident when trying to assert themselves, are lacking in active idealism, leading to a dreamy, lethargic way of life. Any slight mental stress or strain can unbalance them. There is a tendency towards prejudice against strangers, stemming from the fact that Cancerians may lead a relatively sheltered family life, with little contact with the outside world. They may also revel in self pity and lack moral-fibre.

Health Difficulties of the Group

The parts of the body affected by the moon are the female reproductive organs such as the uterus and ovaries. Trouble may also be experienced with the lymphatic and sympathetic nervous systems. Diseases affecting the stomach, liver, pancreas and digestion are prevalent amongst this group. With their great liking for food and drink, Cancerians may suffer from digestive troubles, stomach ulcers, flatulency and dropsy, illnesses that require strict dieting and exercise. Care should be taken to safeguard against such conditions.

Physical Appearance of the Group

They are short and tend to be plump, with a rather kindly, sympathetic expression. The timidity of the subject is reflected in his appearance. Moon-faced, pallid-skinned, they have large, deep-set eyes, usually hazel or grey in colour. They also have rather fleshy hands and feet, pointed chins and noses, and the hair is usually straight and light brown in colour.

Below: *The theme of water pervades Cancer as* **Right** *does Motherhood: this group by J.H. Fonley.*

The Most Suitable Occupations

All nautical, maritime and allied professions are dominant in this group. People who work with liquids such as chemists and publicans are also quite dominant and all work in hotels, restaurants, breweries, waterworks, etc. The clergy in general comes under the influence of Cancer.

Ideal for Success

The Cancerian is a highly receptive, intuitive, rather conservative type. They can be reserved, sympathetic, exceptionally sentimental and highly sensitive, which at times may lead to timidity and even morbidity. The subject tends to incline to moodiness or fickleness. Attempts should be made to cast out all trace of morbidity which usually springs from distrust and suspicion of others. The mind should retain its deep and ready sympathies, whilst functioning on a higher level to attain material gains.

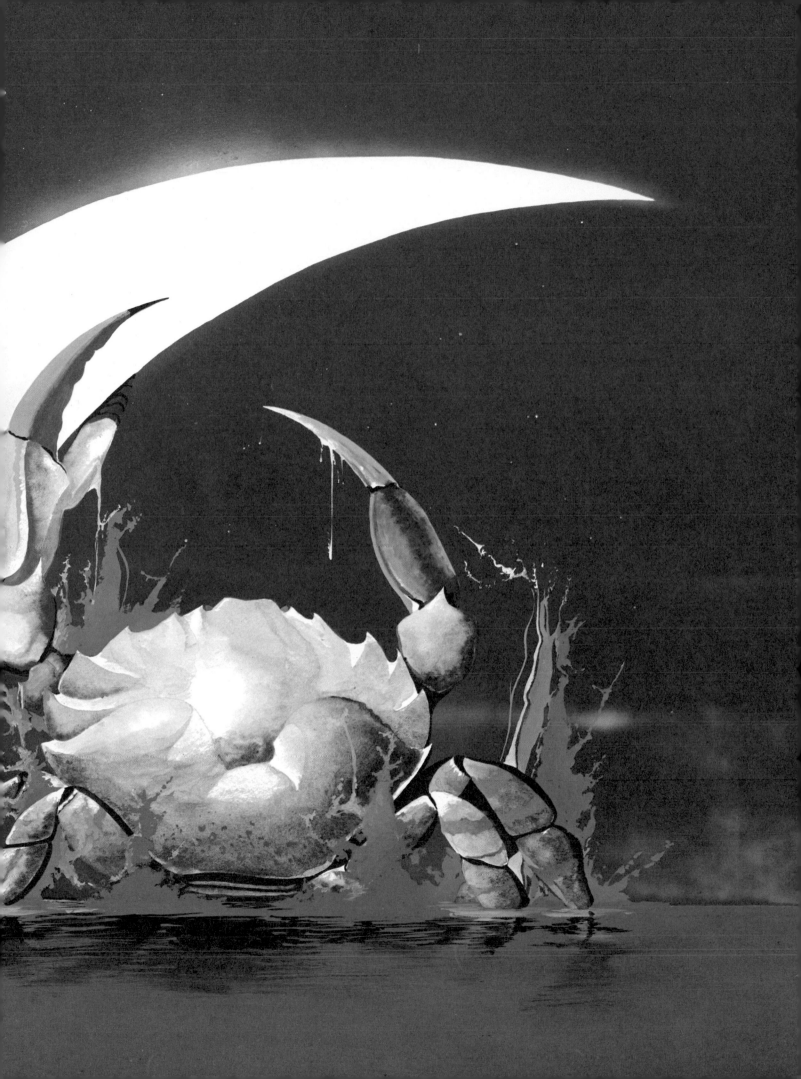

A peaceful river scene; the harmony and tranquility of which makes an appropriate image of the sensitive, nature loving side of the Cancerean personality.

LEO

♌

Leo, the Lion, fifth sign of the Zodiac
July 24th - August 23rd
Self confidence, enthusiasm, pride

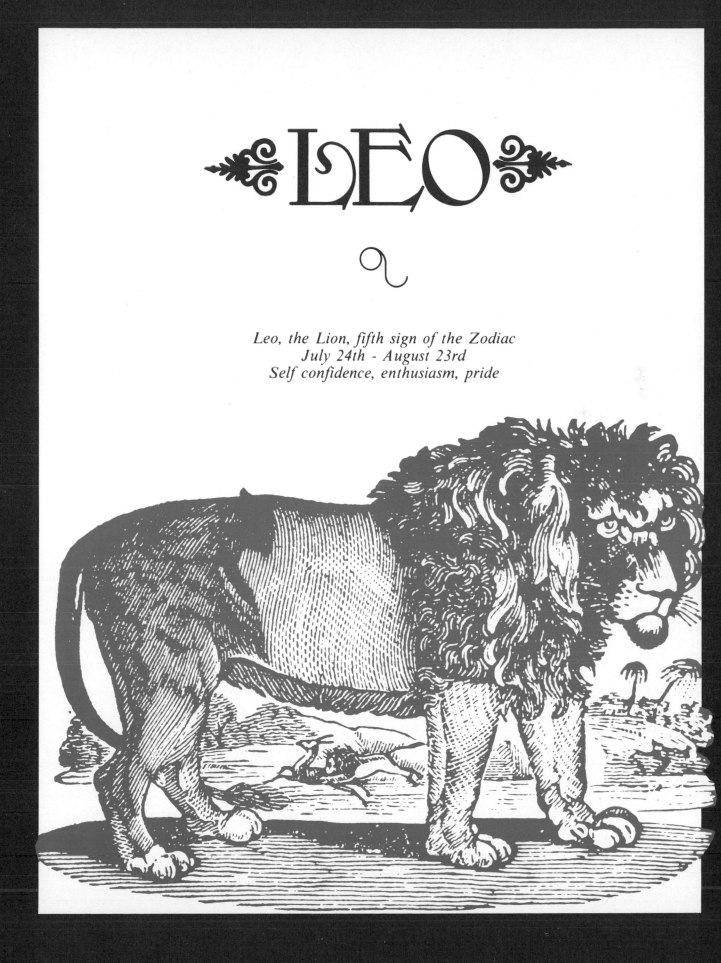

Leo (Positive Sun, Fixed-Fire)

Compatible Signs: Aries and Sagittarius

Advantages of the Group

The Leonian subject is courageous, bold in thought and deed, big hearted, open minded and has a strong sense of dignity. They are eminently suited to positions of prominence and authority. Their open-mindedness is accompanied by kindliness and a great deal of optimism, which are characteristic of their general outlook. They demonstrate great vitality, controlled ambition, fidelity to all causes, dogged persistence, tolerance, humanitarianism, an equable temper, and are very affectionate and brimming with self-confidence.

Disadvantages of the Group

Courage and boldness may degenerate, resulting in the individual becoming something of a despot or tyrant. These become arrogant, boastful and quite ruthless. Being born leaders, the subjects will attempt to be 'boss' whether they have the ability or not. At the same time they may attempt to take the credit for something that a subordinate may deserve. Ostentation, overindulgence, sheer vanity, and pompousness are apt to be in evidence. Their vanity is so great that they dislike anyone who does not wish to flatter them. They cling to established tradition, are very snobbish and patronising and may incline to meanness.

Top: *Leo's association with the sun is expressed in the dignity of this golden boy.* **Left:** *Leo is also linked with children.* **Above:** *Albrecht Durer a Leo subject, typifies the signs characteristics.*

Health Difficulties of the Group

Leo subjects health difficulties may centre around those parts of the body that control the vitality of the individual. Generally, Leonians suffer a great deal from heart diseases and other allied illnesses such as palpitations and fainting spells. Bad circulation may also pose a problem at times. Anaemia and spinal diseases such as lumbago may also be in evidence.

Physical Appearance of the Group

The subject's stature depends on the position of the sun. Sometimes it will be above average height with a well-proportioned, robust body; at other times it may be slim and of average height. They have rather large heads, big staring eyes and large noses. The hair is usually blonde or light brown in colour.

The Most Suitable Occupations

This group is most suited to positions of leadership. Executive posts in all professions will have their fair share of Leonians. Any position where he can assert his authority is ideal, such as top ranking military officers, highly placed civil servants, diplomats and any other government posts. Professions allied to high finance, stockbroking and banking are also suitable, as are principals of schools and universities. The legal profession, any constructive or pioneering work, and any work entailing the use of gold will lead to success.

The Ideal for Success

A generous, tolerant kind of mind that always commands attention and great respect is the gift of the Leo personality. He is a very open minded person who is against any kind of secrecy. He is courageous and bold but inclined to be domineering and even tyrranical when the sign is badly placed. Thus, what he needs is wider expansion, without thrusting his dominant, aggressive will on subordinates or competitors. It would be desirable to preserve a careful equilibrium between the ambitions of the individual and the means he employs to achieve them.

Top: *Leo's are excellent stockbrokers.*
Middle: *Acting and monarchy are associated with the sign, which also governs paddle steamers,* **(Below) Following page:** *The king, bearing gold, totally Leonine.*

VIRGO

♍

Virgo, the Virgin, sixth sign of the Zodiac
August 24th - September 23rd
Discriminative, methodical, logical

Virgo (Negative of Mercury, Mutable-Earth)

Compatible Signs: Capricorn and Taurus

Advantages of the Group

The Virgo group, like Gemini, has great mental dexterity and versatility. It is pre-eminently a sign of a fine discriminatory sense and great critical powers. They are endowed with great intellect and are capable of reasoning out the intricacies of any problem through sheer logic. They are especially precise with regard to minute details, are very neat and methodical and take great pride with their work. They are very attracted to learning and are the easiest sign to educate, consequently they gain insight into difficult problems that subjects of other signs would experience difficulty in trying to solve. They are loyal, charming, tactful, intuitive, honest, artistic, versatile and have good taste with regard to the arts. They abhor pretentiousness and take pride in their work – being always anxious to give good service. They are humorous and although they love work, they prefer to be left alone to do it. In business they are financially cautious.

Disadvantages of the Group

If badly placed the Virgo subject may become distasteful and objectionable. He will treat criticism of his own work with contempt, whilst being a prejudiced fault-finder himself. Narrow-mindedness, egotism and a lack of sympathy for the feelings of other people, may prevail. The mind becomes devious and calculating, and very selfish. They become sarcastic, cantankerous, fuss too much about details, thus obscuring the general picture. Exceptional meanness may turn them into latter day 'Scrooges', arousing the dislike of many people. Officiousness, nervousness, lack of principle, extreme neuroticism and scepticism are common characteristics of the badly placed Virgoan.

Health Difficulties of the Group

The parts of the body more readily prone to infection are the bowels, intestines, liver, abdomen, spleen and the duodenum. Digestion difficulties, constipation and other intestinal difficulties are common complaints of this group. They may also suffer from diarrhoea, dysentery, worms, appendicitis and peritonitis. Nervous disorders may also be in evidence.

Left: *Cornfields have strong associations with Virgo and* **Below:** *The cat, usually thought of as a feminine animal is the creature usually thought to belong to the sign.*

Right: Oast houses are governed by Virgo.
Top: *A cool, white relief by Ben Nicholson.* **Bottom:** *Bees are usually associated with the sign.*

Physical Appearance of the Group
Virgo subjects have an upright appearance with rather a broad head. They have a high forehead, a pale complexion, with generally brown but occasionally blue eyes. The hair is usually brown and is inclined to be curly.

The Most Suitable Occupations
Professions concerning writing and the production of written matter are very suitable, such as journalism, secretarial and clerical work. Occupations that entail the use of the hands such as wood carving, metal working, carpentry, engineering professions and gardening are also favourites of the sign. They often tend to become doctors, psychologists and other allied analytical professions. Other professions which suit them entail abstract, statistical and inventive skills, such as computer programming. They also make very good critics.

The Ideal for Success
The Virgo mind is ever-probing, high intellectual and ingenious. They are fond of detail and hyper-critical when opposed. It is a penetrating kind of mind which should be focussed on one thing at a time instead of many problems simultaneously, to ensure fair criticism and judgement of each individual project. Their hyper-critical side badly needs controlling.

Below: *A maiden at a spring, in a bas relief by R.W. Martin. The maiden is the symbol of Virgo.*

LIBRA

Libra, the Scales, seventh sign of the Zodiac
September 24th - October 23rd
Balance, justice, love of beauty

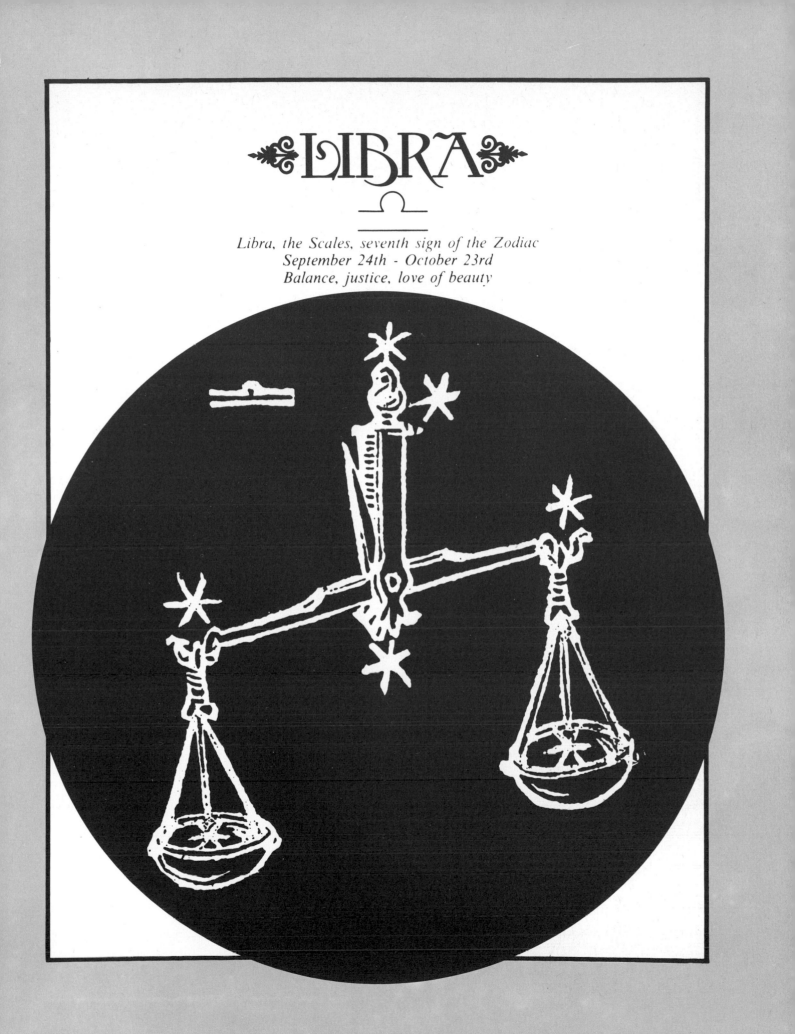

Libra (Positive of Venus, Cardinal-Air)

Compatible Signs: Aquarius and Gemini

Advantages of the Group

Librans have a well-balanced love of harmony and peace and are fanatically in need of harmonious relations with others. They are amiable, courteous, have a great respect for honour, go to great lengths to avoid any friction with people, preferring to use tact and compromise rather than brute force in a face-to-face confrontation. Justice, truthfulness, loyalty and sympathetic attitudes towards the less fortunate, are other fine qualities of this group. They like good company and make good companions themselves, as they are very easy to get on with. They have a balanced intellect, keen appreciative values of beauty, and hold impartial views.

Disadvantages of the Group

Librans demonstrate a measure of procrastination which at times shows them to be slovenly and careless. They frequently give the appearance of being superficial and insincere, due to their dislike of confrontations and a marked preference for compliance or compromise at all costs. This lack of resistance may make them many enemies. Vanity is another of their chief faults. They tend to be garrulous, ostentatious and are forever flirting. They can seldom do things for themselves and nearly always need moral support. They are also ultra-sensitive and their moods rapidly fluctuate between elation and extreme despondence and they can also be rather aggressive and warlike at times. They over-indulge in sentimentality, are often too hesitant or cowardly and seldom make any progress because of their extreme laziness.

Left: *Lancelot and Guinevere; Venus, the ruling planet of Libra exerts a romantic influence;* **Below:** *a love of music is a facet of Libran delight in harmony.* **Bottom:** *China is governed by Libra.*

Above: *A balancing act, typical of Libra.* **Above right:** *Nietzche, a Libran philosopher.* **Below right:** *romantic trou-badours.* **Overleaf:** *the scales of judgement.*

Health Difficulties of the Group

This type does not have a particularly strong constitution. Parts of the body ruled by Libra are the kidneys, loins, lumbar regions, skin surface, the ureters and the walls of the blood cells. Illnesses that afflict the group are kidney diseases such as acute nephritis, lumbago, eczema and other eruptive skin troubles, urinary troubles and diabetic conditions.

Physical Appearance of the Group

The individual Libran is very graceful, with a moderate height and build in fine proportion. Their eyes are usually blue but can sometimes be brown. The hair is invariably light brown or shades of blonde. Pale, marble-like complexions are common in the sign.

The Most Suitable Occupations

Librans can frequently be found in design and allied professions. Diplomatic service and government work demanding good judgement also attract them. They do quite well in the arts, especially literature and the stage and they make excellent dancers, because of their elegant, graceful figures. The law and allied professions, financial fields, architecture, navigation and public speaking – all suit the Libran.

The Ideal for Success

The Libran is a sympathetic, persuasive and tactful type with a highly discriminative, and impartially judicious mind. Hesitancy, though, would appear to be a severe obstacle. On occasions, self-centredness and extreme ruthlessness obscure their great qualities and need to be checked. Hesitancy should be overcome through the adoption of a stronger line of action, thus enabling the mind's judicial function to be more finely developed.

SCORPIO

Scorpio, the Scorpion, eighth sign of the Zodiac
October 24th - November 22nd
Tenacious, secretive, intensely psychic

Scorpio   (Negative of Mars, Fixed-Water)

Compatible Signs: Cancer and Pisces

Advantages of the Group

Those born under this sign are thorough in most undertakings and have a boundless strength of purpose in pursuing any aim or goal. Dignity, determination, tenacity, aggression and the will to dominate are highly developed traits of this group. Being of an intensely emotional nature, the group has strong affections and is deeply sympathetic towards others. Caution is their watchword and is cultivated to an extraordinary degree. They are consequently restrained in manner, but courageous when subjected to physical duress. They are reliable, responsible, logical-minded subjects and are inclined to secrecy. There is a natural interest in the occult, stemming from their secretive nature. Scorpios radiate a personal magnetism unsurpassed by any other group.

Disadvantages of the Group

Caution becomes exaggerated and leads to jealousy and suspicion of everyone; determination degenerates into oppression and tyranny, cruelty and severe aggression. Treacherous, ruthless, forever seeking revenge, vindictive, quarrelsome, bullying and fanatical – all these bad characteristics make the Scorpion the most bloody-minded of the twelve groups. They constantly boast, over-indulge in sensual pleasures, act callously or show complete indifference with regard to the feelings of others and they frequently treat their fellow man with abuse. Their judgement is often very poor and consequently their fine discriminatory powers are misused or obscured.

Health Difficulties of the Group

Scorpio rules the genital organs, pubic and nasal bones, bladder, colon, prostate gland and haemoglobin. Nasal catarrh, ulcers and hernia are common ailments of this group. Other complaints to be found are the contraction of syphilis, scurvy, uterine and womb troubles.

Physical Appearance of the Group

The Scorpion is usually a thick-set, sturdy but strong-framed type. They are inclined to be under average height and usually have swarthy,

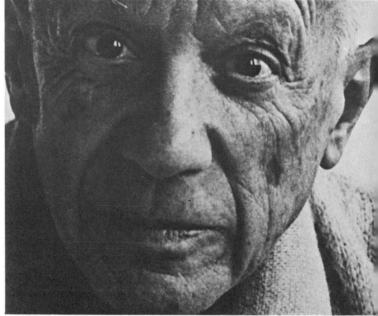
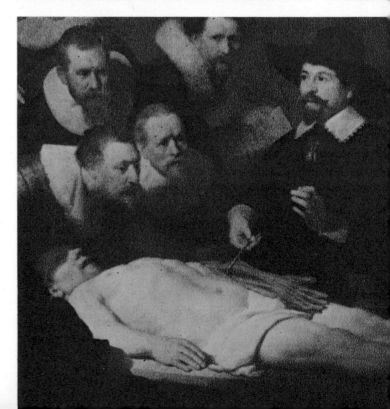

sallow or olive complexions. The eyes are brown and the hair, dark brown or black, is normally quite curly. The nose is frequently aquiline with large nostrils and the chin is small and pointed. The legs may be slightly bowed, but are muscularly built.

The Most Suitable Occupations

Professions where investigational work is needed, such as the police force, detection work of all kinds, private investigators and other allied crime detection work. Being a natural healer, the Scorpion makes an ideal doctor or surgeon. They also make successful livings in the military professions, teaching and chemistry. Many scientists and sportsmen, too, are of this type.

The Ideal for Success

The Scorpion mind is scientifically-orientated but frequently lacks discriminatory powers. Thought processes may be rather hesitant because of the inordinate suspicion and caution of the type. They must eliminate unnecessary caution in order to strengthen their ability to make decisions. The cold, calculating aspect of the nature should be kept well in check. They need to cultivate trust in people.

Opposite Top: *Kim Philby; Scorpio is associated with spying and detective work.* **Middle:** *Picasso; his enormous energy and great sexual attraction make him typically Scorpio.* **Bottom:** *Scorpio's are known to be great doctors and healers.*

This page above: *snakes are associated with Scorpio.* **Below:** *graveyards and death and* **Right:** *spiritualism, are attributes of the sign.*

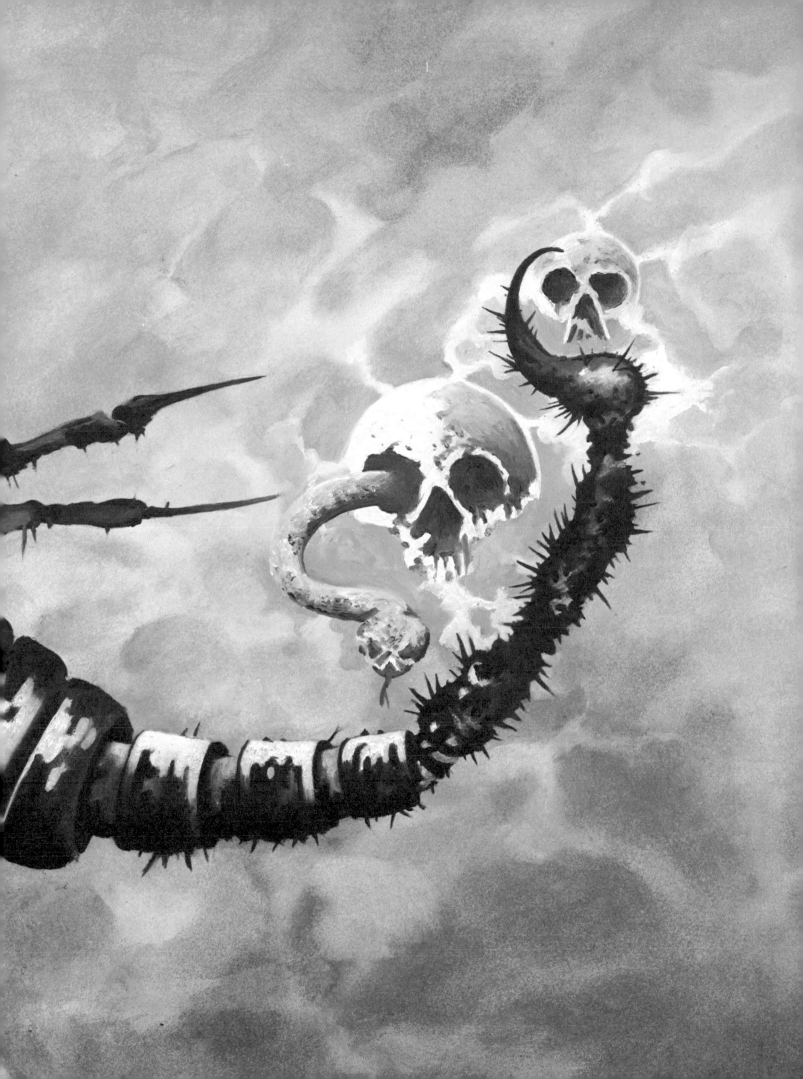

Below: *The intense, highly psychic and secretive Scorpio nature often makes the subject interested in the occult and witchcraft.*

SAGITTARIUS

$\nearrow$

Sagittarius, the Archer, ninth sign of the Zodiac
November 23rd - December 21st
Extrovert, optimistic, independent

Sagittarius

(Positive of Jupiter, Mutable-Fire)

Compatible Signs: Aries and Leo

Advantages of the Group

Sagittarians are born extroverts. They enjoy life to the full and take great delight in all sporting activities. They have a keen sense of sportsmanship, making the group extremely likeable since they seldom make enemies. They are generally optimistic and independent, frank, honest, athletic, hold strong views on personal freedom and have above average mental abilities. They are religious, love travelling, are impulsive and have a generally light-hearted attitude towards life. Their vigour of personality, abundant supply of energy and love of 'fair play', most certainly makes them one of the most popular groups.

Disadvantages of the Group

The chief faults of the Sagittarian are false pride, over-extravagance due to a basically generous nature, lack of tact in their dealings with others and physical over-exertion due to their sporting nature. The subjects, being extroverts, may grow braggardly, boastful, inclined to gross exaggeration, dishonest, arrogant and may also lack personal integrity. They may be quarrelsome and argumentative and tend to revolt against the establishment. As with the Gemini subject, Sagittarians tend to know a little of everything and seldom have a comprehensive knowledge of any one subject, but unlike the Gemini, there is little care over detail. They love being the centre of attraction and are continually trying to impress.

Left: *Sagittarius is traditionally connected with hunting and.* **Below left:** *with archery.* **Below:** *it is the sign most associated with philosophy. The great philosopher Bertrand Russell is a Sagittarian.*

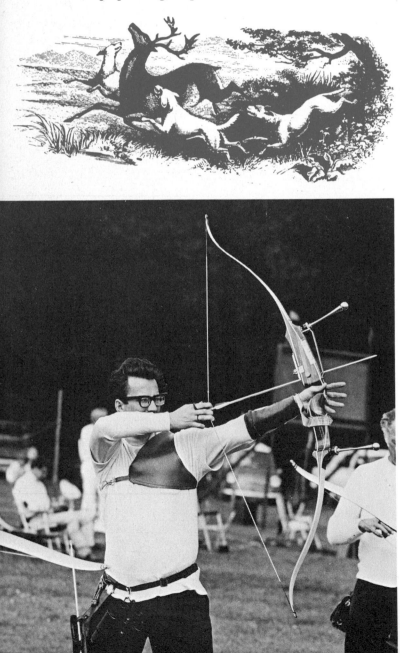

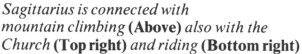

Sagittarius is connected with mountain climbing (**Above**) *also with the Church* (**Top right**) *and riding* (**Bottom right**)

Health Difficulties of the Group

The main parts of the body ruled by Sagittarius are the hips, the thighs, the loins, femur, iliac and sciatic nerves. Rheumatism, rheumatic fever and similar complaints are common ailments of the group. Sciatica and hip diseases may also be prevalent. Because of their strong attachment to sports, Sagittarians are much more prone to accidents than subjects of other groups.

Physical Appearance of the Group

Sagittarius is a tall, athletic, well proportioned type. The face is oval with a high forehead, expressive eyes which are grey and sometimes blue. The nose tends to be aquiline and hair is usually sandy or light brown and is often thin.

The Most Suitable Occupations

Sagittarians gravitate to most sporting or outdoor professions, and often become travellers, explorers and hunters. They also make good philosophers, teachers, clergymen, public speakers and bankers. They could succeed as merchants, civil servants and a large proportion enter the law professions, often making fine judges and magistrates.

The Ideal for Success

Sagittarians have a carefree, extroverted nature. The mind is highly intelligent, if rather flamboyant in expression, and the subject is in general, rather a benevolent, charitable sort of person. The ideal for success would be to channel energies in one direction at a time, thus ensuring the right choice of an objective. Restlessness and lack of concentration need to be firmly controlled.

CAPRICORN

♑

Capricorn, the Goat, tenth sign of the Zodiac
December 22nd - January 20th
Hardworking, meticulous, persevering

Capricorn
(Negative of Saturn, Cardinal-Earth)

Compatible Signs: Taurus and Virgo

Advantages of the Group
Under this sign, we have the diligent, hard working personality. The Capricornian is very ambitious – probably more so than any other group – authoritative and very cautious. They are emotional with an exceptionally kind and humane disposition. Thrifty, persistent, self-disciplined, meticulous, introspective, loyal, tactful and materialistic – these characteristics are all very prominent in the sign. Their materialistic gains – which usually result in the subject accumulating great wealth – are the results of hard work and patient efforts. The Capricornian tends to stick to old habits and customs and dislikes change intensely. Their diplomatic manner in dealing with others makes them good politicians and tacticians. Perseverance, great concentration, prudence and great care are noticeable traits of their nature, and their massive industry often brings this group into prominence and notice.

Disadvantages of the Group
The subjects have a tendency to extreme pessimism. They never seem to see the good side of anything but prefer to look at the dark side of life. Theirs is a gloomy outlook, continually worrying about irrelevant matters, frequently affected by fluctuating moods and they are often difficult people to please. They tend to love being dominant and are often too self-important and snobbish. They dislike being ignored and become very arrogant and bigoted about settled convictions. Their sympathies are limited and they have very little heart which usually leads to sheer cruelty and selfishness. There is a prominent tendency to use other people for their own advantages or gains, revealing a strong streak of cunning. They tend to live in the past and this refusal to progress limits their abilities and capabilities. Restlessness, unscrupulousness, narrow-mindedness, envy, inflexibility and bitterness are fairly common in these subjects. They are, in fact, very ineffective people.

The influence of Saturn, the oldest of the planets gives Capricorn associations with Father Time (**Below left**) *and old age* (**Below right**)

Health Difficulties of the Group

The parts of the body ruled by Capricorn are the knees, joints, hair and the skin. Dislocation of bones, articular rheumatism and cramp are common ailments of the subjects. Breakages of bones are frequent. Syphilis, eczema and other allied skin complaints also affect the group. Toothache is a regular, minor complaint.

Physical Appearance of the Group

A tall, lank, loose jointed type, the build is slighter than average. A narrow chin and lantern jaw enhance the features. The nose is large, straight and prominent, and the complexion is dry and sallow. The eyes are generally blue and the hair light-coloured but sparse.

The Most Suitable Occupations

Work of a routine or organisational nature such as clerical and allied office employment attract Capricornians. Estate management, the building trade, agriculture and farming occupations also have their fair share of the sign. There is a tendency towards religion in the group, resulting

Above left: *A coal mine in the Rhondda Valley. Capricorn is traditionally associated with underground work like mining.* **Above:** *The jolly Father Christmas is a lighter Capricornian image.*

in many entering the church. Most branches of engineering and also occupations requiring discipline, such as the armed forces and the police forces are suitable for them.

The Ideal for Success

The mind, at its best, is quite forceful, but is frequently unbalanced by the intense degree of caution cultivated. Clear, concentrated thought, love of method and a commanding power of self-control, enhance the fine qualities bestowed on the native. He may, however, tend to be self-centred, pessimistic, lacking in concentration and without sufficient sympathy and tact towards his fellow being. What is needed here is the cultivation of tolerance to all people and all things on a wider scale. Concentration should also be encouraged and ambition should not degenerate into unscrupulousness.

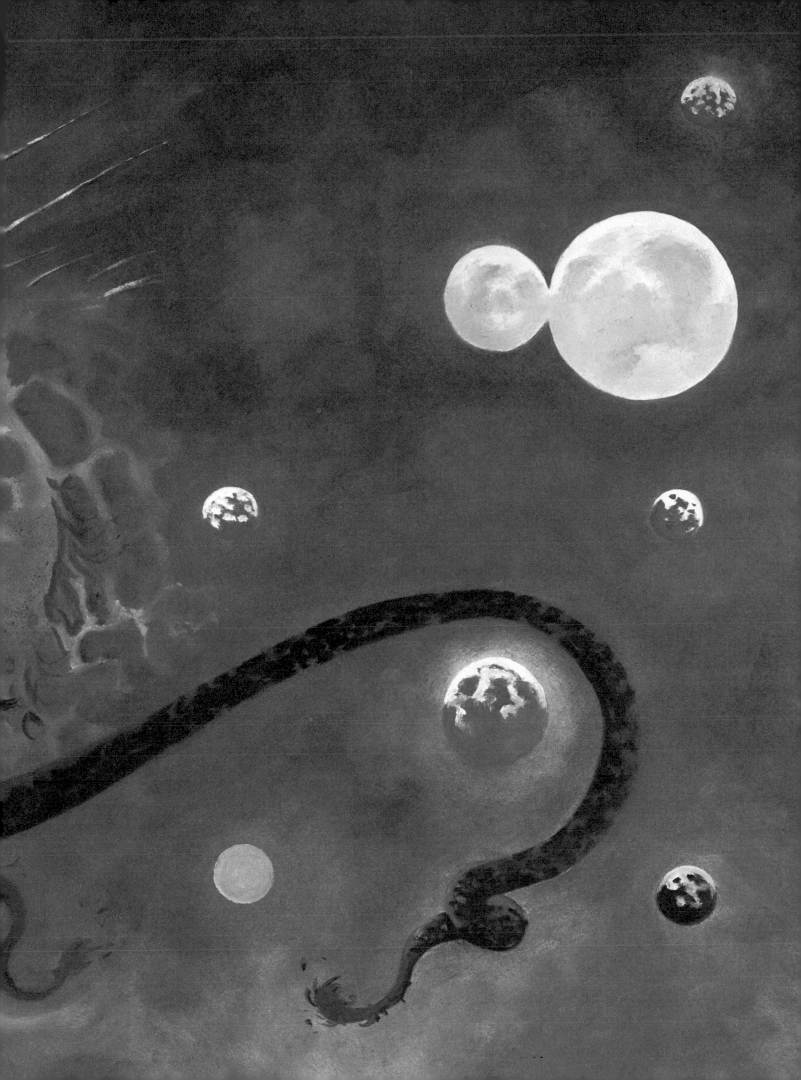

The element earth is strong in the Capricornian make up and may be responsible for the traditional association with caves.

AQUARIUS

≋

*Aquarius, the Water Bearer, eleventh sign
of the Zodiac, January 21st - February 19th
Tolerant, helpful, idealistic*

Aquarius (Positive of Saturn, Fixed-Air)

Compatible Signs: Libra and Gemini

Advantages of the Group

Aquarius is the sign of humanitarianism. The subjects are utterly truthful, kind, sympathetic, patient, sincere, friendly, faithful and affectionate. The Aquarian resembles the Capricornian in his serious outlook when the influence of Saturn is strong, but becomes more unconventional, independent and rebellious towards enforced obedience and conformity when the influence of Uranus prevails. Aquarians are very stable and are unperturbed in times of a crisis. They are tolerant, helpful and idealistic – and often become leaders and reformers. Flexibility of mind, intelligence, above-average creative ability, a progressive outlook, deep sense of kinship with his fellow man and clarity of vision – these characteristics are all finely balanced in the Aquarian subject. It is the symbol of mankind and some of its finest traits.

Disadvantages of the Group

Being more idealistic than practical, the Aquarian may lack common sense. This may lead to indecision, dreaminess, diffusion of actions and practical incompetence. They become disorganised, disorientated, erratic, unreliable and exceptionally impressionable. They lack self-control, become sceptical, are far too conscientious and worry a great deal. They may lack moral fibre, leading to cowardice, bad judgement will prevail and there will also be a distinct lack of consistency and forthrightness, leading to hypocrisy and slyness.

Health Difficulties of the Group

The parts of the body mainly afflicted are the calves, ankles, teeth, general circulation and nervous system. Bad circulation, neuresthenia and other nerve disorders and blood disorders are common illnesses prevalent in this group. Varicose veins, elephantiasis, damage to ankles and legs and a sensitivity of the lower body in general. Toothache, pyrrhoea are other minor ailments that afflict the group.

Below left: *Karlheinz Stockhousen combines interest in electronics with aesthetic inventiveness, typically Aquarian.* **Below:** *incense and censers are thought to be special to Aquarius.*

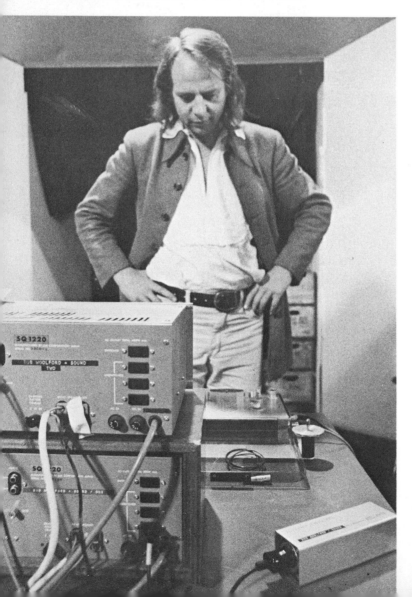

Physical Appearance of the Group

They have a handsome, pleasing appearance, with tall well-formed bodies. The skin is pale and usually of good texture, the chin is prominent, and there may be a high, wide brow. The head is quite large, the eyes brown or blue and the hair is a light coloured shade of brown. Aquarians have an unassuming, kindly demeanour and appear to be very helpful.

The Most Suitable Occupations

Being of an intensely scientific nature, Aquarians tend to gravitate towards trades associated with electricity and radio. They make good technicians in radio, television and computer fields. They also make good journalists, actors and writers because of the imaginative side of their nature. Aviation and associated professions, religion and other professions that safeguard humanity, and any occupation where the use of their inventive ability is called upon bring out the best in the subject.

The Ideal for Success

The mind is scientific and inventive with finely balanced powers of reasoning. The subject is kindly, tolerant, optimistic and diplomatic in his view of life. There is some fixity of ideas, a lack of foresight and a general slowness in attitude, making it difficult for the group to make hasty decisions. What is needed is for the mind to be trained to concentrate more before any measure of success can be achieved. Their practical abilities also need developing.

PISCES

Pisces, the Fish, twelfth sign of the Zodiac
February 20th - March 20th
Imaginative, peace loving, kind

Pisces (Negative of Jupiter, Mutable-Water)

Compatible Signs: Cancer and Scorpio

Advantages of the Group

The Pisces character resembles the Aquarian, sharing similar humanitarian traits. They are pure idealists and spend their life supporting and helping good causes. This is at once evident by the range of wide sympathies nurtured in the character. They are very imaginative, full of inspiration, warm-hearted, peace-loving, have the ability to make great personal sacrifices, are receptive to the emotions of others and are spiritually motivated. They are full of understanding and forgiveness but they are themselves often misunderstood. The Piscean has all the abilities to advance himself, but as with the Aquarian, he finds practicality difficult to attain. Consequently he is seldom a very strong character. Sensibility, great intelligence, amiability, the power of interpretation, inspiration and affection for animals are noticeably prominent characteristics. Pisceans make very good listeners and being happy and convivial by nature, make very good companions.

Below: *The dreamy Piscean is usually interested in and influenced by spiritualism and the occult and is often a natural medium.*

Disadvantages of the Group

The group frequently lacks the ability to make decisions or to concentrate on matters in hand. They have little common sense and a general ignorance of ordinary values. Their oversensitivity produces moods that fluctuate rapidly between elation and deep depresssion. This lack of balance often leads to the subject being spendthrift, unmethodical and procrastinative. Diffidence, religious hypocrisy, hysteria, secrecy, masochism and deception are all bad Piscean traits. They suffer from guilt complexes, an inability to express themselves clearly, and often degenerate into severe alcoholism and become far more impressionable than is really healthy. They also may become drug addicts, due to the Piscean's eternal need for emotional or physical stimulation. Ideas become too scattered, and consequently misunderstood or obscured, and they generally become far too anxious about life. It is not surprising that a large percentage of suicides originate from this group.

Health Difficulties of the Group

Pisces rules the feet, toes, foot muscles and bones, liver, clotting mechanisms and blood circulation. Diseases that prevail are those that affect the feet and toes, such as bunions, corns and gout. Influenza and colds are also fairly prevalent. Tumours, dropsy and liver diseases

such as cirrhosis occur when there has been an excessive intake of alcohol. Heart trouble may be present.

Physical Appearance of the Group

Generally Pisceans are below average height but well-proportioned in shape, possibly with a heavy build. The complexion is bright and may be rather fleshy. The eyes are usually brown, and the hair is all shades of brown. They are often snub-nosed, but more frequently aquiline in appearance. The subjects have large, liquid eyes and the face is rounded.

The Most Suitable Occupations

Pisceans gravitate to maritime professions and all trades that have connections with liquid. They are often seamen, medical practitioners and chemists. Entertainment and the more sober branches of art, literary, religious and philosophical professions are well represented

Top left: *The expressive face of Piscean dancer Rudolf Nureyev. Pisces is connected with Abbeys* (**Left**) *and dreams* (**Above**)

by this group. Psychology, public house management and work where the imagination is called upon, are other trades that attract Pisceans. Prison service is also a popular choice of profession amongst the group.

The Ideal for Success

The Piscean mind is very puzzling. Idealistic, extremely romantic, highly imaginative and creative, extremely sympathetic, they lack the ability to be practical. In many cases they are completely ignorant of worldly matters and wander around like lost souls. What is needed for success is a balance to effect the perfect equilibrium of the mind's great imaginative powers and creative ability with an equally strong practical and forceful quality.

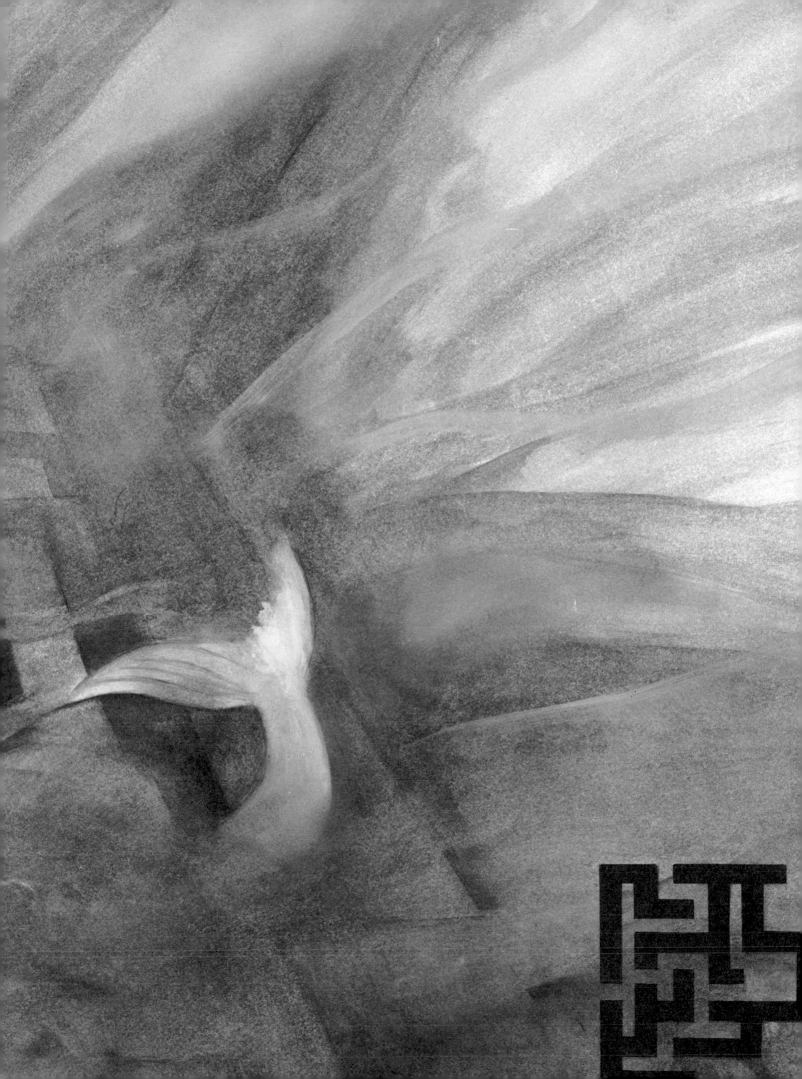

The major Piscean image is the Fish, painted **Below** by W.M. Scott.

Bottom: *An aerial view of the Goodwin Sands, beautiful, always shifting, sometimes dangerous.*

THE LIVING ZODIAC

PRACTICAL ASTROLOGY

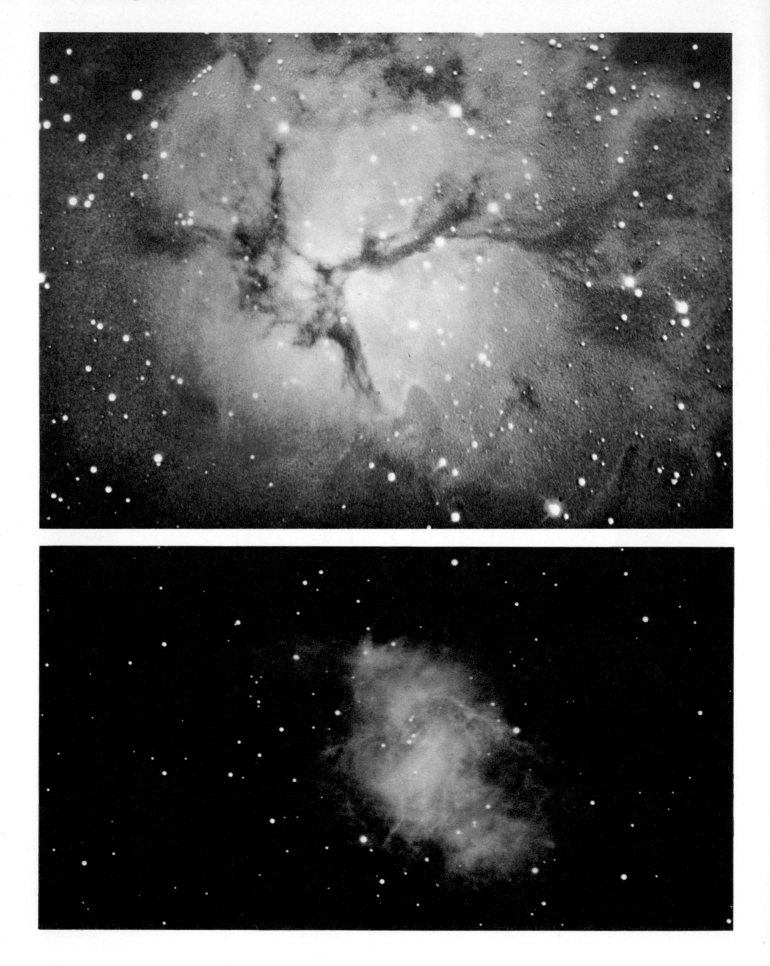

Now to look at the sky itself. The Zodiac is seen through the telescope instead of through the mythological vision of astrological tradition, though they still retain their allusive names. **Opposite above:** *The trifid mist in the galaxy Sagittarius. A mass of gas and dust 32,000 light-years away, it contains many hot newly-created stars.* **Opposite below:** *Hydrogen represents over 90 per cent of all the matter in the universe. It is the main constituent of stars and huge interstellar gas clouds such as the Crab Nebula.* **Above left:** *The spiral mist in the constellation Canes Venatici is 10 million light years away. Such nebulae are clouds of diffuse gas within the Milky Way system of stars.* **Above right:** *A radio telescope view of the seven Sisters. Pleiades is a star cluster within the constellation Taurus, about 300 light years from the solar system. Nebulosity is probably caused by rarefied matter made luminous by radiation.* **Left:** *The Andromeda galaxy among the stars of the Milky Way contains 100,000 million stars, and 100,000 light years in length, it is the only extra galactic object visible to the naked eye.*

Table of Aspects with their recognised Symbols

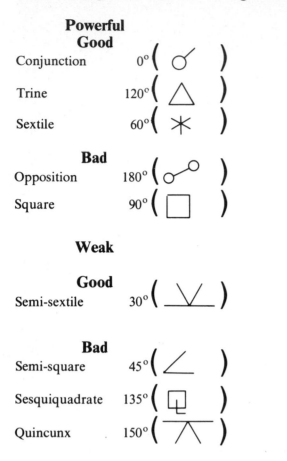

Powerful

Good

Conjunction	0°	☌
Trine	120°	△
Sextile	60°	✳

Bad

Opposition	180°	☍
Square	90°	□

Weak

Good

Semi-sextile	30°	⋎

Bad

Semi-square	45°	∠
Sesquiquadrate	135°	⊡
Quincunx	150°	⚻

There are other aspects which we can obtain from dividing the circle of 360° by 5, the most notable aspect being the Quintile which is an angle of 72°. Multiples of the Quintile are:

Biquintile	– 144°
Decile	– 36°
Tredecile	– 108°
Vigintile	– 18°

These aspects are all very weak but are considered harmonious.

The benefic aspects, Trine, Sextile and Semi-Sextile, are obtained by dividing the circle by 3, 6 and 12. The aspect conjunction is obtained when there is no distance between the two planets in the zodiac. They may either be close together in one sign or at the end of one sign and at the beginning of another. In conjunction, the influences of the planets are mixed. Thus we may either get a harmonious influence with favourable planets (i.e. Jupiter and Venus) or obstructive influences with bad planets (i.e. Mars, Saturn). It should be remembered that aspects are really strong only when conjunct, trine, sextile, square and in opposition. The reader should now commence to use the symbols, and become quickly familiar with them. When two planets are in the same distance from the Celestial Equator, this is called the Parallel of Declination (P). It doesn't matter whether both bodies are north, one is north and one south, or whether both are south. As with two planets being in conjunction, the Parallel of Declination is a powerful aspect when formed between two benefic planets (Jupiter, Venus), or a benefic and a neutral (Sun, Moon, Mercury), and not very good when formed between a benefic and a malefic (Mars, Saturn, Uranus, Neptune and Pluto). Between malefics and neutrals they are considered obstructive but there may be modifying factors. Two malefics are a bad aspect and need careful consideration.

It must be remembered that aspects are seldom the exact angle. For instance, two bodies may not be exactly in opposition (180°) but may be a few degrees out (say 176°). This angle of effect is called the Orb. It must be remembered that the more exact an aspect is, the stronger the aspect, but the planets are allowed to move within varying orbs. Influences will be felt within the orbs of those planets. The orbs themselves vary from planet to planet, and astrologers differ as to the distance that the effects of the orbs will be felt. Here are the orbs as generally accepted for each of aspects.

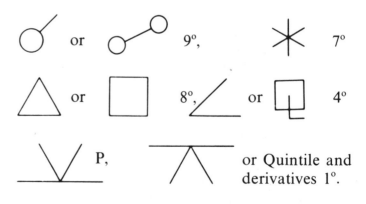

For the Asc. or M.C. (Midheaven) about 5° is the maximum allowed.

Opposite page: *A medieval astrolabe. The astrolabe was an essential piece of equipment for all astrologers until the eighteenth century; before the days of easily available ephemerides it was necessary to plot the aspects for each case, an extremely precise calculation.*

Table showing imaginary aspects on the Ecliptic

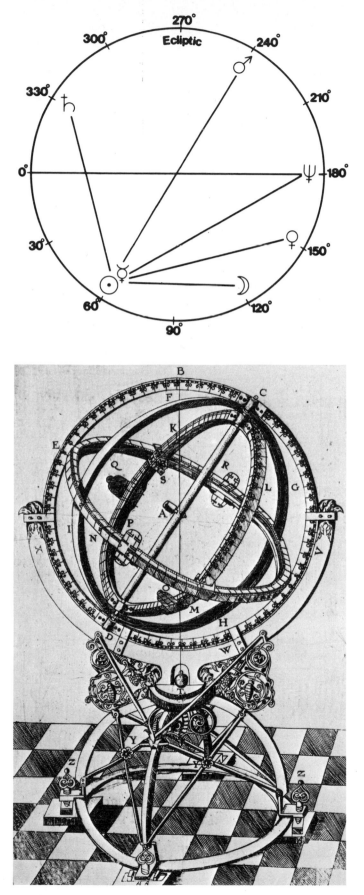

Using the symbols of the planets and aspects, we can see that:

$$☿ ☌ ☉, ☽ ⚹ ☉, ♂ ☍ ☉, ♄ □ ☉, ♀ □ ☉, ♆ △ ☉$$

Signs, themselves, can be in aspect as you will see when realising that qualities are in square and elements are in trine. From this you will realise that if a body were in Aries and also a body were in or near the same degree of Libra, these two bodies, as the signs themselves, would be in square. Further, if there were a body on or near the same degree of Leo or Sagittarius (with Aries, comprising the three fire elements), the two bodies would also be in trine. Aspects should be learned by looking at the signs which contain the bodies. The longer method would be as follows. Commence with the planet nearest 0° of Aries and count the number of signs to the second body. Thus if in this case the first planet were in Aries and the second body were in Gemini, we would count two signs forward from Aries. These two signs would equal 60° (12 signs, total 360° – 30° each sign). Take the exact position of the second body, say 14° 29′ of Gemini, and add together.

60°	
14°	29′
74°	29′

From this subtract the position of the first body, say 12° 15′

74°	29′
12°	15′
62°	14′

Thus we see that this is within the orb of the trine, which is 8° either side.

Significance of Planetary Aspects

In interpreting a chart, the astrologer will have to use his skill and judgement to decide what aspects are going to be harmonious and which are going to be obstructive. Below we give some planetary aspects and what they traditionally signify, however it must be realised that in drawing other conclusions, an astrologer will not necessarily be wrong in his assumptions.

A Selection of Planetary Aspects

⊙△☽, ⊙✳☽

The sun is representative of life, energy and vitality. The moon is symbolic of protective instincts, moods and enthusiasm. Both the aspects signify a sincere, loyal type of person; honest, radiating exceptional vitality and very popular with a zest for living. Indicative of good chance of success for an individual.

⊙♂☽

The aspect of neutrals conjuncting is favourable. There may be a tendency for the subject to be over-sensitive and of a temperamental disposition. However his general vitality of character is assured.

⊙☐☽, ⊙♂☽

Obstructive aspects. Life will be full of barriers and obstacles. Frustration will be obvious in the subject. He is likely to be influenced or dominated by the mother in early life. The

Above: *The photographs show three stages of a partial eclipse of the sun which took place on 20 July 1973. An eclipse could have a great influence on a horoscope.*

subject may be easily offended and hard to please. Generally the character will be unhappy with his lot. The constitution may be prone to constant illness.

⊙♂☿

This is a favourable aspect. The subject will be a good, clear, logical thinker. Self-expression will come very easily to him and he will have the ability to learn rapidly. There may be a certain amount of self-centredness though. The Sun and Mercury are never in obstructive aspect as their orbits never take them outside 30° of each other.

⊙△♀, ⊙✳♀

These aspects will produce a colourful, sympathetic, artistic and refined person. They will

As the sun's brilliance diminishes its importance as source of all energy and life on earth becomes apparent. The primitive fear of an eclipse is easy to understand.

be pleasant and well liked and will have an air of distinction about them.

⊙ ☌ ♀

A favourable aspect. Cultured, happy, and nearly always popular. The effect of influences of conjunct aspects if approaching nearer than 3° to the sun is swamped by the sun's influence.

⊙ △ ♂, ⊙ ✶ ♂

Forceful, energetic, full of initiative, powerful and vital. The natives will be forthright, outspoken, have a great deal of personal integrity and luck and will more often than not refuse to be opposed. There may also be a lack of tact.

⊙ ☌ ♂

The subject will tend to be over-impulsive, sel-

fish, tactless, rude and boastful. He may lack practical ability in decision taking.

⊙ □ ♂, ⊙ ☍ ♂

The energy, courage and vital forces that motivate the subject degenerate to tyranny, explosive temper, selfishness and a particularly violent disposition. He may be quarrelsome and may pick on people who cannot stand up to him. Destructive and completely unreasonable, the subject may be an obnoxious, difficult person to get on with. Likely to suffer from unfounded persecution complexes.

⊙ △ ♃, ⊙ ✶ ♃

Possibilities of great success in the native's chosen profession. Honest, forthright, wise, authoritative and just. A good boss who treats his employees with the kindness and respect that befits them.

⊙ ☌ ♃

A favourable aspect. Wisdom and kindliness in the native.

☉□♃, ☉☍♃

The subject is liable to be a quarrelsome, arrogant, brash sort of person. He makes a tyrannical boss.

☉△♄, ☉⚹♄

Hard work will reap the deserved rewards. Effort will result in the achievement of goals or aims, in the latter half of the life of thc native. Appreciative, careful, healthy and with character and a vital personality.

☉☌♄

Depression, repression and persecution complex. Ambition channelled in wrong directions, possibly with calamitous results. Native is of good executive material.

☉△♅, ☉⚹♅

A progressive sort of person with an inventive, ingenious and logical mind. This may be channelled into literature or art.

☉☌♅

Inspiration of the better variety, which is usually sensibly motivated. Impulsive and over-sensitive. Always coming up with new ideas.

☉□♅, ☉☍♅

Inspired but has no practical ability to carry out new ideas. Unconventional, constantly changing his mind and job, a rebel against the established norm, lacking in self-discipline and given to frequent whims.

☉△♆, ☉⚹♆

Religious, philosophical and supremely scientific. Likes his comfort.

☉☌♆

Inclined to secrecy. Possible interest in the occult. The subject may very well have psychic powers if the sun falls in any of the water signs or Aquarius.

☉□♆, ☉☍♆

Possibly a drug addict. Curious or likes to probe. Sexual aberrations amounting to perversion. Fascination with poisons. In need of mental and physical stimulation.

☽△☿, ☽⚹☿

Witty, clever and a liking for languages. A great deal of travel either for pleasure or for work, may be involved.

☽□☿, ☽☍☿

Tends to worry too much. Over-sensitive, unreliable, pays too much attention to detail, indecisive nature and is the sort who is always starting but never completing new projects. Possibly a hypochondriac. Inclined to be a bit overwrought and hysterical.

☽△♀, ☽☌♀

Good artistic taste, sound discriminatory powers. Interest in the arts may be strong and practical. Chance of success may be greater than most.

☽□♀, ☽☍♀

The character is careless and lacks finishing ability. Tends to leave projects only half completed. Not a good opportunist. Changeable, fickle minded.

☽△♂, ☽⚹♂

A go-ahead type. Ultra-sympathetic and easily shocked and horrified. A sporting type with good business instincts.

☽☌♂

Go-ahead, rugged, rough-and-tumble qualities. Good health and general constitution. Rashness or inclination to take unnecessary risks.

☽□♂, ☽☍♂

Impulsive, impudent type of person. Tends to be tyrannical, boasting, bullying and lacking in self discipline. Courageous sort.

☽△♃, ☽⚹♃

The native will be honest, outspoken and forthright. The influence of Jupiter produces a measured amount of success in chosen fields.

☽□♃, ☽☍♃

Moon's influence retards progress. Foolish speculation, financial loss, and loss of reputation. Judgement becomes unbalanced leading to bad mistakes in choice of business partners.

☽△♄, ☽✱♄

The effect of the moon is to bring about change, but Saturn provides stability. Loyal, level-headed person. Great care is exercised before entering into any venture. Trusted by everybody. Great powers of concentration and philosophical outlook. Very responsible type of person.

☽☌♄

Bouts of depression. The native appears to be a mournful sort of character. Aspect not too bad.

☽□♄, ☽☍♄

Pessimistic sort of person. Never sees the good side of things, always the black. Distrusts everyone. Unenterprising, inflexible, bitter sort of character. Unpopular.

☽△♅, ☽✱♅

Eccentric sort of subject. Always desiring new changes. Always seeking new friends, new ideas. Women may be flirts while men may be philanderers. Inventive type of mind. Interest in the occult and the mystical. An imaginative and interesting type of person.

☽☌♅

Inclined to lack moral fibre. May be a little too amorous or even erotic. Generally a harmonious aspect.

☽□♅, ☽☍♅

A bohemian. Constantly changing and constantly on the move. Often seeking out the weird and the odd. Egocentric, with misplaced pride.

☽△♆, ☽✱♆

Artistic nature prominent when both planets well aspected. Love of music and the stage. Sensitivity, intuition, vivid imagination, refinement, and a keen appreciation of beauty in all forms. There may also be a passion for travel.

☽☌♆

The subject may be very highly psychic. Foresight and clarity of vision, to the extent that the subject may be prophetic.

☽□♆, ☽☍♆

The dreamy type, produced by the moon's instability and the inconsistency of Neptune. Tends to live in a permanent dream world. Dishonest to a degree. Possibly adept in black magic and other branches of the occult.

☿☌♀, ☿✱♀

Refined, harmonious, pleasant, cheerful, witty, likes the good life, keen appreciation of beauty, especially where art, literature and the stage are concerned. Easy learner and great mental dexterity. If Mercury is strong, the leaning is to literature, writing and travel, if Venus is strongly aspected, there is more of an inclination to the arts and entertainment fields. Mercury and Venus never in Trine. Widest angle between them is about 75 degrees.

☿△♂, ☿✱♂

Great mental dexterity and energy. Logical, clear mind with finely balanced debating ability. Ability to reach conclusion promptly. A fine discriminatory and analytical mind. Success is readily achieved in this type of person.

☿☌♂

Far too energetic, and far too impulsive. A favourable aspect if both planets well placed.

☿□♂, ☿☍♂

Energy and mental dexterity mix badly producing a person of sarcasm instead of wit. They incline to be argumentative instead of reasonable, plan things badly and tend to leap before looking, consequently finding themselves in difficulty. Incompetence seems to be characteristic of them.

☿△♃, ☿✱♃, ☿☌♃

A person of great tolerance, respect for the law, harmonious, sound judgement. They are generous and honest and usually have clear logical minds.

☿□♃, ☿☍♃

Judgement becomes unsound and the intellect reveals only superficial knowledge of subjects. Erratic attitude, that can cause serious legal disputes. A possibility that the character may be libellous.

☿△♄, ☿✱♄

Generally slow, but sound workers. Deliberation is a watchword. Usually clear, logical thinkers, unlikely to be perturbed. Great determination and the will to succeed – but at his own pace. Truthful, trustful and completely reliable.

☿ ☌ ♄

Possibly a pessimistic type of person. Inclines to be a bit meek and introverted.

☿ □ ♄, ☿ ☊ ♄

Problems appear to be much larger than they really are. Bitterness, fear that he won't succeed in a project and indecision are rife. This type must not be trusted with secrets.

Below: *Medieval bible illustration of the creation of the heavens. Jehovah holds the sun and moon in either hand:* **Opposite:** *Blake's gnostic vision of creation, Nobodaddy with his dividers.*

☿ △ ♅, ☿ ⚹ ♅

An inventive mind. Always looking for new interests, new companions. Keen intellect, and good, sound logic. Good aspect for an interest in astrology and related subjects. This is due to the combination of mental dexterity and natural curiosity.

☿□♅, ☿☍♅

The sort of person who seeks out the unusual. Exceptionally eccentric. Possibly perverted.

☿△♆ ♀⚹♆

A vivid imagination. Eloquent and intellectually brilliant. Cheerful, witty and very good company. Psychic if both planets are well aspected.

☿□♆, ☿☍♆

Mental dexterity is obscured by the vivid imagination, sometimes leading to dreaminess. Lack of logic and clear, lucid thinking. Dishonest and untruthful, and a noticeable lack of concentration where important matters at hand are concerned.

♀△♂, ♀⚹♂

An ambitious, lovable type. A great deal of charm, refinement and wit, and is the type that is everybody's favourite. Over-generous nature.

♀☌♂

Acts on impulse. Either likes or dislikes you intensely on first sight. Affection degenerates to the sensual pleasures.

♀□♂, ♀☌♂

Sensuality gets out of control, a lack of moral fibre being noticeable. Bad tempered disposition, possibly violent, extremely jealous, coarseness of character.

♀△♃, ♀⚹♃

These subjects like their own types. They have well balanced, just minds. Refinement of taste, extremely courteous and completely selfless.

♀□♃, ♀☍♃

Unfair to his close ones. Attempts to buy friends. Over-extravagant, slovenly in judgement, lacking in foresight where speculation might be concerned. Infidelity where loyalty should be most important.

♀△♄, ♀⚹♄

Sound, practical judgement, simple-minded, full of integrity, knows how to budget wisely. Not quick to show affections, but when he does they are sincere and immovable. Grit and determination, and the will to succeed at all costs.

♀☌♄

The type that is completely faithful and loyal to the end. Not quick to show any affections though. The sort of person who makes a first class friend but a pathetic lover.

♀□♄, ♀☍♄

Impotence or frigidity may be in evidence. Virility dies away and causes deep depression. Usually engaged for many years and the choice of a marriage partner is usually disapproved by the family. Age differences in the partners are not uncommon in this sort of subject. Indecision, frustration and a pathetic air about him. Wife possibly a hypochondriac.

♀△♅, ♀⚹♅

A magnetic personality. Falls in love on the spot. Very artistic, usually exceptionally original and unconventional. Fickleness in tastes. Sudden gains.

♀□♅, ♀⚹♅

Divorced quickly after swift marriage. No due care and consideration about the feelings of others. Holds exaggerated views.

♀△♆, ♀⚹♆, ♀☌♆

Artistically inclined, especially in music. Makes friends with his own kind. Colourful personality who stimulates the opposite sex.

♀□♆, ♀☍♆

The kinky type who likes to attract bad characters. Makes friends with unreliable people. Deceitful, unfaithful, disloyal. Cause of bad scandal, and adverse publicity.

♂△♃, ♂⚹♃

A champion of law and order. Advocate of fair play and deadly foe of injustice. Law abiding, honest, just and open minded. Make very good leaders, especially in the armed forces. Strong sense of patriotism and duty.

♂☌♃

Badly placed, planets will produce a type that is apt to try to deal out justice himself. Takes the law into his own hands. An indication of great wealth, although this will not smooth out difficult situations.

♂□♃, ♂☍♃

Bad judgement. Over-frivolous with money, often in financial difficulties, quick tempered, over impulsive. Judgement is obscured by personal whims.

♂△♄, ♂⚹♄

Great tenacity and strength of purpose. Practical, courageous, vigilant, diligent, honest, and brimming with confidence. This type make good soldiers and solicitors.

♂☌♄

Saturn slows down, holding back and preventing the subject going ahead swiftly with enterprises. The subject may become downhearted and despondent, selfish, and there may be a tendency towards tyranny or extreme cruelty.

♂□♄, ♂☍♄

Cold, calculating, cruel, selfish, with complete disregard for the feelings of others. They continually make enemies and cannot be trusted. They are always suspicious and do not trust anyone. There do not appear to be any mitigating circumstances in the callous nature of the subject.

♂△♅, ♂⚹♅

An inventive type, where full use of the abilities are made. A purely constructive, positive type. Always taking the initiative.

♂☌♅

Extremely unusual and eccentric type. Inventive powers and good stamina. A tendency to enter projects without due care and consideration.

♂□♅, ♂☍♅

Powerful, but lacks initiative or practical ability. Stubborn to extremes, unpredictable. There does not appear to be any real sense of purpose in this group.

♂△♆, ♂⚹♆

An enthusiastic approach to the occult and all things mystical. Tend to become medical practitioners. This type may well be drug abusers. Enthusiastic and boundless energy.

♂□♆, ♂☍♆

A destructive type of person tending to be vindictive. Usually mixes with the wrong company and is a wandering type, unable to settle. There is a marked lack of concentration.

♃△♄, ♃⚹♄

A very trustworthy type. Sincere, frank, honest and very stable. Success will come – regardless of the retarding effect that Saturn has on the character. There is fine judgement and discrimination in all matters.

♃☌♄

An honest, stable, reliable subject, but likely to be of a sober, sombre disposition, with no joviality or conviviality about the character. Thorough and deliberate in all he does.

♃□♄, ♃☍♄

Saturn throws off the impact of Jupiter's sound judgement and just nature. The subject may become over-cautious, and suspicious of everyone and everything. Makes many enemies which is not surprising considering his lack of tolerance and his extremely pessimistic attitude.

♃△♅, ♃⚹♅

The mind is of a supremely inventive nature. Jupiter being wise and fair, and Uranus being inventive and unusual, novel ideas and vivid imagination may lead to the bizarre. The subject may be worldly wise, humane and very original.

♃□♅, ♃☍♅

Erratic character. Likely to lose large amounts of money in speculation. Not very practical. Maybe gets the wrong side of the law, through his own lack of judgement.

♃△♆, ♃⚹♆

Jupiter gives wisdom and good judgement, Neptune gives mystical and psychic qualities and consequently the occult is a centre of interest for the subjects. Intuition will bring success for speculative ventures. They gravitate to maritime professions such as working on ships. Love of beauty is in evidence.

♃☌♆

Favourable aspect. If Jupiter is badly aspected the subject may be speculative and have ideas that do not materialise.

♃□♆, ♃☍♆

The sound judgement of Jupiter is obscured by

the Neptunian mystic, psychic or fantasy quality. Subsequently the subject may be slightly superstitious. Occasionally on the wrong side of the law. A supporter of crank movements, that frequently lead nowhere and are more trouble than they are worth.

♄△♅, ♄⚹♅
An inventive mind. The determination and will to succeed coupled with strong concentration ensure some measure of success.

♄☌♅
Possible over-eating, causing some ill health, but generally a good aspect.

♄□♅, ♄☍♅
A "Walter Mitty". A vivid imagination bordering on the fantastic. Inventive powers obscured, and ideas frequently lead nowhere. Self-centredness and extreme eccentricity. Exceptionally bad tempered.

♄△♆, ♄⚹♆
Deep, concentrative powers. Tendency towards all things psychic.

♄☌♆, ♄□♆, ♄☍♆
Meddling in psychic and occult matters that can be dangerous. Bad speculation. Disloyalty by friends. A little unbalanced or deranged.

♅△♆, ♅⚹♆
People interested in the occult and astrology. Espionage, bizarre or secretive activities.

♅☌♆, ♅□♆, ♅☍♆
Experimenting with the occult can be dangerous. The subject is probably unstable, and maybe thrives on this. Success and failure come just as easily. Moody and very individual.

The Twelve Houses

The Houses are the division of the horizon above and below the earth into 12 equal parts, as with the zodiac. All aspects of human life are, to some extent, governed by one or more of the houses. The houses relate more to the material aspects of life rather than to the spiritual. As will be seen, the positions of the houses have a marked effect on the individual. They should be considered along with the Sun signs.

The 1st House
The first house rules the individual. It rules the physical body – character, appearance, individuality and health. It conveys some idea of the way the individual is motivated in thought and deed. The first house affects the living body, both physically and mentally, as it manifests itself.

The 2nd House
The second house rules the material possessions of the subject. It governs financial affairs and dictates income, expenditure, financial ability in money matters, profit and loss.

The 3rd House
Governs four aspects of life – communication, travel, relatives and the mind. It is especially concerned with blood relations. Brothers, sisters, aunts and uncles will be shown here. Also all aspects of writing and communications such as books, correspondence and letters. Short-distance travel is encompassed by this house, also work and education.

The 4th House
Encompasses the parents and the home. Influences that affect an individual such as close family are especially strong. Being a water sign, the 4th house has great significance. It may indicate a happy, stable home or, as may be the case, a broken home. It indicates all that is private, secluded and withdrawn. It rules land, housing, the father (more so than the mother) and is indicative of the conditions of the latter part of one's life.

The 5th House
This house has great significance for leisure, pleasure, love and the birth of children. It also influences all sorts of speculative activities, holidays, whether for business or pleasure, enterprising ideas and affections. In the latter case it may be affection for people, animals or friends. Sexual drive and desire can be estimated from the position of the planets at the time of birth. This may indicate overt indulgence, sensuality, lust, and may indicate a lack of moral fibre. Being in trine to the first house, it is considered a house of good luck.

The 6th House
This house covers two aspects of life; health and work. The joys and pleasures of the 5th house

are said to be the outcome of the work completed as indicated by the 6th house. It is also indicative of health and the general state of the native's constitution. If the health is good, they can face any obstacles encountered. This also encompasses the likelihood of any operations likely to be undergone, any diseases likely to be contracted, favourable dietary indications and the physical size of the native. It also rules the native's relationships with subordinates, inferiors, servants and actual service. And it also governs his prospects as an employee – indicating possible promotion. Being associated with fluctuating moods and dispositions, the house is considered as being obstructive. Benefic or neutral planets may be weak and malefic planets subject to erratic moods. If the native undergoes a period of bad health, it will be indicated here, also the severity of the illness will be shown.

Below: *The Earth, the seasonal occupations, and the signs of the Zodiac. This woodcut is taken from an early sixteenth century English translation of the* Shepheards Calender, *and is a delightful example of its kind.*

The 7th House

This house deals with marriage and business partnerships, possible enemies and competitors. The influence is generally good as it shows husbands, wives, co-operative or congenial partners and friends. If badly placed, this may turn into direct competition or even open hostility. Dangers to be avoided and advantageous chances will be indicated in this house.

The 8th House

This is the house of death, wills, legacies and, to some extent, health and well-being (including accidents). It may be significant of the way the subject will die, indicating a peaceful or violent death. It is symbolic of the death of the old and the birth of the new. It governs the goods and chattels of the deceased – wills, legacies and inheritances in particular. It shows debts, warns against financial speculation, while indicating favourable times to gamble or speculate. If a planet is near to the cusp of a house it could indicate the physical size of a person. It encompasses general well-being and the effect friends, partners and casual acquaintances can have on the native's constitution with regard to contamination and infection. It also rules the funerary trades, such as undertaking and grave digging, and any occupation that is concerned with death. One's sexual nature and inclinations may be prominent.

The 9th House

This house rules religion, philosophy and travel. All aspects of travel are included in this house – showing whether the native dies in his homeland or abroad, whether he will emigrate or not and the purpose and outcome of journeys of any great length. It is related to the spiritual side of man, in that it will indicate that all is concerned with religion in the subject. Hypocrites will be easily identifiable. It rules the philosophic side of man – all that is concerned with speculative and inspired thought. It is connected with the clarity of visions and foresight that one associates with prophetic types. Also this house rules all aspects of the Church and the law.

The 10th House

This house encompasses the vocation and social standing of the native. It is indicative of professions to which a native would be best suited. It may also be indicative of those people who exert a great deal of influence over the subject, especially the mother. The house rules the native's social position or status.

The 11th House

This house encompasses the hopes, ambitions and aspirations of the individual, and indicates whether they will be fulfilled or not. There will also be an indication of the type of friends it would be best to make and also the type of friends *not* to make. Whether these acquaintances will be to the native's benefit or will be likely to be obstructive or harmful influences, will be very clearly indicated. This house is considered beneficial.

The 12th House

This is the house of betrayals, ambushes, ordeals, secret enemies, misfortune, sorrow, confinement and illnesses. This is popularly called the "Hell of the Zodiac". The house warns the native about opponents of all kinds, and how to handle them. If involved in law suits, it will indicate whether or not the native will win them. The house indicates whether sadness is caused by himself, or by his association with others. It is the house of loss, disappointment, personal sacrifice and illness, which may lead to confinement for some length of time. The house also encompasses any connections the native might have with institutions such as hospitals and prisons, and will indicate whether the connection is an employee or as an inmate.

Observations on the Houses

The twelve houses can be divided into two distinct parts. Houses 1 to 6 are mainly concerned with you, as the individual, whilst houses 7 to 12 mainly concern other people. With houses, an orb of between $4°$ and $6°$ either side of the cusp is permissible. This may, of course, connect two houses. If a planet is at the end of one house and near the cusp of another house, the planet's influences may affect both houses. The work of the houses is mainly concerned with the fate of an individual (as opposed to the character).We can now show a figure showing, Signs, Houses,

Opposite: *The Moon and the activities under its government. The Moon governs Cancer and appropriately the picture is dominated by water. From a series of woodcuts of the planets by Hans Sebold Beham 1500-1550.*

Luna.

Qualities, Elements, and the polarity of signs, showing that no two houses are the same.

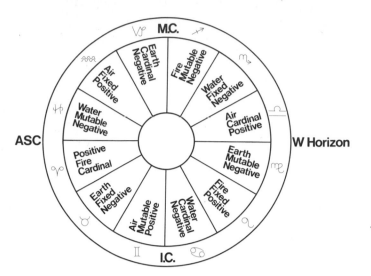

From this it can be seen that signs or houses in square always have opposite polarities, signs or houses in trine have the same polarity, and signs or houses in opposition are of the same polarity.

The Horoscope

Setting up a Horoscope
The data required for this operation is:
(a) Date, place and time of birth;
(b) An astronomical ephemeris which indicates the positions of the planets at any given time;
(c) A table of houses for the latitude of the place of birth;
(d) A horoscopic diagram.

The setting up of a horoscope involves two processes. The first is the calculation of the Sidereal time of birth (commonly called S.T.) or the Right Ascendant of the Midheaven (M.C.). This, as we have already explained earlier, is measured along the Celestial Equator from 0° of Aries. From this we obtain the houses, in which we insert the planets whose positions are obtained from the Ephemeris. Most Ephemerides (the plural of Ephemeris) are calculated for G.M.T. (Greenwich Mean Time), but it must be remembered to deduct one hour for B.S.T. (British Summer Time) and two hours for D.S.T. (Double Summer Time came into operation during the period of the Second World War) if either of these times were in operation at the time of birth.

For example, for someone born at 3.30 p.m. on July 29th, 1973 in London, B.S.T. was in force, so for horoscopic purposes we deduct one hour to give us 2.30 p.m. G.M.T. We now come to the question of converting 2.30 p.m. G.M.T. into S.T. We open the Ephemeris to the month and year we require. We are concerned with the bottom half of the left hand page, in this case. The first two columns are the days of the month and the day of the week, and the third column, which is what we are concerned with, is headed Sidereal Time. We must point out here that this is the S.T. on the M.C. for noon each day. This point must be remembered as it is very important at this stage. Copy down the S.T. for the *first* noon that *precedes* the birth of the subject. In the case of our example, which is 2.30 p.m., the S.T. will be for noon on the 29th July, 1973. Let us now complete the conversion. We have a birth at 3.30 p.m. on July 29th, 1973. What is the S.T.?
(a) Deduct one hour from the time given as B.S.T. was in force.

Below: *The horoscope of George, Duke of York second son of Edward VII. When this horoscope was published in 1867, his elder brother was heir, though the astrologer forecast that he would become George V. In fact he did, for his brother died before him.* **Opposite** *Mercury, and the activities under its government, such as the inventive sciences.*

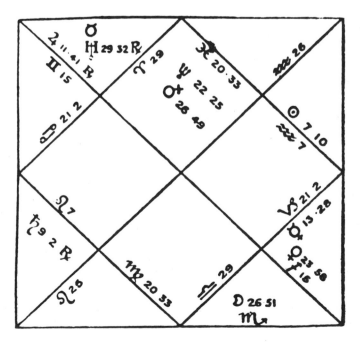

Mercurius.

(b) Turn to relevant page in the Ephemeris and read the S.T. for noon first preceding the birth time of the subject, which in this case is 8 h 27 m 59 s.

(c) To the S.T. obtained from the Ephemeris, you add the hour of birth, thus:

h	m	s
8	27	59
2	30	0
10	57	59

In the case of someone being born at 3.30 a.m., the procedure is the same.

(a) Correct for B.S.T. – 2.30 a.m.

(b) S.T. for noon first preceding birth. In this case, this will be noon on the 28th July, 1973. So we have a S.T. of 8 h 24 m 3 s. 2.30 a.m. on the 29th July, 1973, is 14h 30m 0s later so we add the two times together in exactly the same way.

h	m	s
8	24	3
14	30	0
22	54	3

If this time should ever *exceed* 24 hours, you *always* take 24 hours from your total and that is your answer. There is now one minor alteration to make. S.T. differs from G.M.T. in that there are approximately 3m 56s more to a sidereal day, i.e. 24 th G.M.T. – 24h 3m 56s S.T. The birth times we have added to the S.T. are G.M.T. so we must correct for S.T. The amount we add is 9.86 secs for every hour. Thus for 2.30 p.m., as in the first case (the p.m. birth), we add 2.5 × 9.86s. This equals 24.65s (25 to the nearest) and this we add to our final S.T. of 10h 57m 59s. This gives us a final total S.T. of 10h 58m 24s. In the case of the birth time of 2.30 a.m. we add 14.5 × 9.86s = 2m 22.9s (2m 23s to the nearest) to our S.T. of 22h 54m 3s, giving us a final S.T. of 22h 56m 26s.

We now come to the questions of longitude (distance in degrees East or West of the Fixed Meridian, Greenwich). The rule in this case, is simple. If the place of birth is due *East* of Greenwich, you *add* 4 minutes for each degree of longitude. If the place of birth is due *West* of Greenwich, you *subtract* 4 minutes for each degree of longitude. For example, given that Paris is longitude 2° 20′ East of Greenwich, you would add 4 mins x 2⅓ = 9m 20s to the S.T. Or, given that Sheffield is 1° 30′ West of Greenwich, you would subtract 4 mins. x 1½ = 6m from

your S.T. Always remember, though, to convert to G.M.T. from B.S.T., D.S.T., C.E.T. (Central European Time) or any other local time that might be in force. We can now dispense with seconds, which are not necessary in converting to S.T., except in special cases. S.T. is usually converted to the nearest minute. In the case of making up birth charts of people abroad, using other than G.M.T., the first step is to convert the time in force to G.M.T. and then find the S.T. in the Ephemeris for the date and time of birth. For example, we have a child born in New York, 22nd February, 1973 at 4 a.m. What is the S.T.? We find that New York uses E.S.T. (Eastern Standard Time) which is five hours behind Greenwich, so this is equivalent to 9 a.m. G.M.T.

	h	m
S.T. for noon, 21st Feb, 1973.	22	5
Add 21 hours (First noon – 12 noon 20th Feb.)	21	0
	43	5
Subtract 24 hours	24	0
	19	5
Correction from Clock time to S.T.		3
	19	8
Correction for longitude of New York. Subtract for due West 75°	4	56
S.T.:	14	12

Further examples are unnecessary since this conversion to S.T. from a birth anywhere in the world, is quite simple. All one needs to do is to follow the rules:

(a) Reduce to G.M.T. from B.S.T., D.S.T. or whatever the regional standard time.

(b) From that G.M.T., obtain your S.T. for the noon *preceding* the birth of the subject – remembering to correct from clock time to S.T.

(c) Correct for longitude east or west of Greenwich – adding for a place due East, subtracting for a place due West.

Insertion of Planets

We now come to the task of plotting the planetary positions, which presents no difficulty.

Opposite: *Venus and the activities under its influence. The licentious side of Venus is shown here, although it is often expressed as a love of beauty and the arts.*

Venus.

The position of each of the planets in the Ephemeris are given for 12 noon G.M.T. What we must do is to find the daily motion of the planets if the birth of the subject is before or after noon G.M.T. Obviously with slow planets such as Neptune, Uranus, Saturn and Jupiter, this daily motion can be quickly calculated, but for the other planets it is a longer job. If in an example of a birth 3 p.m., January 29th, 1973, we want to find the position of Mercury, the method is as follows. Turning to the relevant page of the Ephemeris, we see that on the 29th January, 1973, Mercury is 9° 54′ ♒ and at noon the next day it is 11° 38′ ♒ So the daily motion of Mercury can be said to be 1° 44′. The distance the planet would travel in three hours would be 1° 44′ divided by 8 = 13′ which is *added* to the noon position of 9° 54′ ♒ thus making Mercury's position 10°o 7′ ♒ If the birth were before noon, the 13′ would be *subtracted*.

It is advisable, however, when seeking the position of an individual planet, to use the logarithmic tables in the back of the Ephemeris. For example, what is the position of Mars on April 10th, 1973 at 2.25 p.m.? At noon, Mars is 10° 23′ ♒

The daily motion is 43′

Log. 43′	1.5249
Log. 2h 25m	0.9970
motion of Mars in 2h 25m = 4′ =	2.5219

Therefore the position of Mars at 2.25 p.m., 10th April, 1973 is 10° 23′ + 4′ = 10° 27′ ♒ Planets and angles need only be calculated to the nearest degree in the case of the cusps of succedent and cadent houses, and to half a degree in the case of angular houses.

A sample horoscope

We shall draw up a Horoscope for 1.10 p.m., March 13th, 1973 at London.

	h	m	s
S.T. for Noon, March 13th:	23	23	55
Add Birth time:	1	10	0
Correction for clock time to S.T.:			12
	24	34	7
Subtract 24 hours:	24	0	0
		34	7

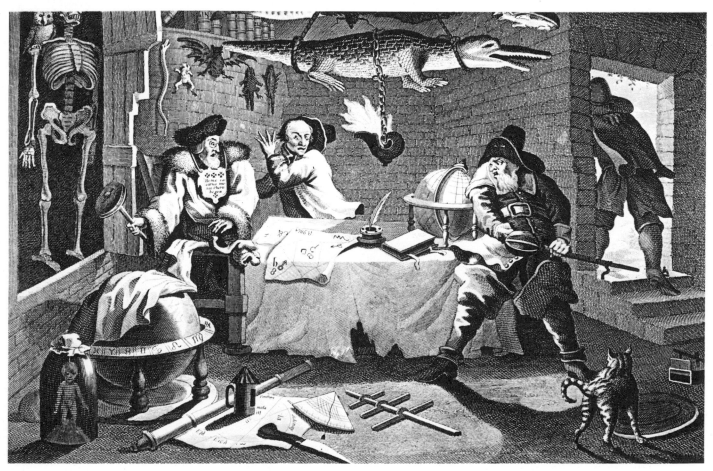

Opposite: *An engraving by William Hogarth illustrating a passage from Butler's satirical poem* Hudibras *in which the villain attempts to cast a horoscope, with much mumbo-jumbo.*

Above: *A plaque attributed to Martin Didier, depicting Neptune on his sea-horse drawn chariot. Neptune is the ruling planet of Pisces, and of course is the god of the sea.*

Firstly, in the table of houses, we find that 33m 4s is very near to our 34m 7s. Therefore we enter the Ascendant at 3° ♌ in our chart. The system used here is known as the 'Equal House' system, which is accredited to Ptolemy. We next have to plot the position of the planets.

We take the log of the Greenwich time (1.3133) and to this we add the log of each planet's daily motion. This will give the motion of each planet in 1h 10m and this added to the planet's noon position on March 13th, 1973, will give us the planet's positions in our diagram at birth.

(a) Daily motion of the Sun = 1° (to nearest)

	Log.
	1.3802
Log. 1h 10m:	1.3133
	2.6935

Thus converting this figure back to degrees and minutes in the log tables, we find this gives us 3′ which is added to the sun's noon position at 22° 46′ ♓, giving birth position of the planet as 22° 49′ ♓

(b) Daily motion of the Moon = 13° 54′

	0.2372
Log. 1h 10m:	1.3133
	1.5505

This gives us 40′ which is added to the moon's noon position of 13° 42′ ♋ giving a birth position of the Moon at 14° 22′ ♋.

(c) Daily motion of Mercury = 57′

	1.4025
Log. 1h 10m:	1.3133
	2.7158

This gives us 3′ which is *subtracted* from Mer-

Above: *Another view of the Sun with the dominant Lion, from Sacrobosco* Sphaera Mundi.

cury's noon position of 23° 27′♓, giving the birth position of Mercury as 23° 24 ♓ The reason for this substraction should be explained. The planets' movements should follow the same path as the signs move through, i.e. anti-clockwise. Sometimes, they appear to slow down, stop, then carry on with their normal orbit. This is called Retrogression (R.) and all planets are retrograde at times, with the exceptions of the sun and moon.

(d) Daily motion of Venus = 1° 15′   1.2833
           Log. 1h 10m: 1.3133
                               2.5966

This gives us 4′ which is added to Venus's noon position of 15° 52′♓, giving a birth position of Venus at 15° 56′♓.

(e) Daily motion of Mars = 42′   1.5351
           Log. 1h 10 m: 1.3133
                               2.8484

This gives us 2′ which is added to Mars' noon position 20° 32′♑ giving us a birth position of Mars at 20° 34′♑.

Jupiter, Saturn, Uranus and Neptune move very slowly, and consequently can be calculated at a glance. Jupiter's daily motion is 12′. 1h 10m is about one-twentieth of 24 hours, and so one-twentieth of 12′ is about three-fifths of a minute, so will be taken as 1′ to the nearest. Therefore Jupiter's position at birth will be 1′ added to his noon position of 3° 40′♒ which is 3° 41′♒ The daily motions of Saturn, Neptune and Uranus are so slight as to be completely ignored and so the noon positions for these planets remain unaltered. The positions are:

    Saturn 14° 21′   ♊
    Uranus 22° 11′ ♎
    Neptune 7° 26′ ♐

We now have one more small detail to go

Below: *Venus was supposed to rule the domestic Taurus by day, the romantic Libra by night.*

into. This is the question of house division. Our ascendant, obtained from the Ephemeris, is 3°♌ which is the cusp of the 1st house. The rest becomes a matter of plotting the cusps of the houses at 30° intervals along the circumference of the Asc. For instance, in the case of our example, we find from the Ephemeris that the cusp of the Asc. is in 3° of ♌ to the nearest degree. Thus we can now set up our chart, putting in the tables. The 1st House, i.e. Asc., commences at 3°♌ the 2nd House cusp is 3°♍ the 3rd House cusp is 3°♎ etc. This will give us the 12 Houses, each of 30° each.

We can now plot the planets on the chart. We already have worked out the positions for 1.10 p.m. March 13th, 1973, which are:

Sun	:	22° 49′ ♓
Moon	:	14° 22′ ♋
Mercury	:	23° 24′ ♓
Venus	:	15° 56′ ♓
Mars	:	20° 34′ ♑
Jupiter	:	3° 41′ ♒
Saturn	:	14° 21′ ♊
Uranus	:	22° 11′ ♎
Neptune	:	7° 21′ ♐

These planets are plotted directly on to the diagram.

Diagram of a Chart with Planets plotted

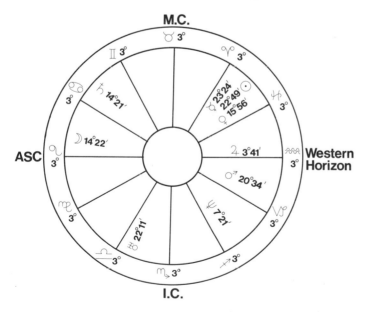

We can now attempt to detect the aspects. Since we are using the 'Equal House' system, and detecting the aspects by counting the signs between planets, there is less danger of making

mistakes – as would occur with other methods of house division. Let us now table again, the symbols of the chief aspects, but this time supplying all symbols of all aspects of planetary significance.

Conjunction ☌
Trine △
Sextile ⚹
Semi sextile ⌄

These we know are benefic aspects.

Opposition ☍
Square ◻
Semi-square ∠
Sesquiquadrate ⊔
Quincunc ⊼

These are the malefic aspects.

Below: *Mars: the warlike ruler of Aries*

⊥ We also have: Semi Quintile (Both weak but considered benefic)

±	Biquintile
P	Parallel of Declination
D	Declination
R[1]	Retrograde
Stat.	Stationary planet
☽☌●	Eclipse of the Sun
☽☍☉	Eclipse of the Moon

The reader need not worry himself too much about the last section. It cannot be stressed enough, though, that one should get used to using the symbols for aspects and not the names of the aspect.

Notes:
All the same Qualities are in Square; All the same elements are in Trine; Fire and Air signs are in Opposition or Sextile; Earth and Water Signs are in Opposition or Sextile.

Retrograde activity
Retrograde activity is said to weaken the aspects of a planet. In fact this action may diminish malefic influences as well as diminish benefic influences if this is the case. It may be that as a planet moves retrograde (i.e. clockwise), so that its motion concurs with the diurnal motion, the effects of the planet may be beneficial.

Southern Latitudes
When working of a chart of someone born in Southern Latitudes, there are two amendments. First, working as before, add 12 hours to your time. Secondly, when inserting the degrees and signs given in the ephemeris on your chart, completely invert the chart, i.e. Instead of Leo being the Asc., make Aquarius the Ascendant, and so on round the chart.

Aspects for the sample horoscope
We should now be in a position to detect and tabulate the aspects of our example.

☉ is ☌	☿	i.e. only 1° away	
☉ is ☌	♀	i.e. only 7° away	
☿ is ☌	♀	i.e. only 7½° away	
☉ is ⚹	♂	i.e. ♂ in	♑
☉ is ⚼	♅	i.e. ♅ in	♎
☉ is ☍	☽	i.e. ☽ in	♋
☿ is ⚹	♂	i.e. ♂ in	♑
☿ is ⚼	♅	i.e. ♅ in	♎
♀ is △	☽	i.e. ☽ in	♋
♀ is ⚹	♂	i.e. ♂ in	♑
♀ is □	♄	i.e. ♄ in	♊
♃ is ⚹	♆	i.e. ♆ in	♐
♂ is ☍	☽	i.e. ☽ in	♋
♂ is □	♅	i.e. ♅ in	♎
♆ is ☍	♄	i.e. ♄ in	♊
☽ is ⚺	♄	i.e. ♄ in	♊

The Judgement of a Horoscope
Although there are basic rules to follow in making a judgement of a horoscope, it is a skill that cannot be communicated in instant terms.

Left: *Saturn is the ruling planet of Capricorn and Aquarius, always shown as an old man; some astrologers believe that the Aquarian age will be the winter of the universe.*

Right: *The astronomer and the philosopher are engaged in discussion; above them are drawn the spheres of the planets and the fixed stars.*
De Concordia astronomical, *Venice, 1490.*

With experience, the apprentice astrologer will begin to find that the factors in an individual horoscope begin to blend together, even if he is faced with two identical horoscopes, of people born at the same time. He will begin to have definite feelings, intuitions which will lead him to different conclusions that he would expect from reading a text book on the subject, and eventually he will learn to trust these intuitions. There are some fortunate people who we could describe as born astrologers, people who seem to have an immediate and instinctive sense of what a horoscope is saying. Basically, the reading of a horoscope depends on the astrologer's capacity to hold together a group of numerous facts, many of which seem to contradict one another, but which ultimately make a clear overall picture. One of the dangers is sticking too closely to the text book, and doggedly trying to fit in every minor detail of the horoscope, when he would do far better to try to find the outstanding features, to get a clear picture in his mind.

There are a few ground rules to keep in mind however. Firstly, it must always be remembered that an individual who is born under a particular sign of the zodiac may be a very atypical native of the sign, so that the astrologer should give up any bias towards reacting primarily on the basis of the sun sign. Naturally the sun sign will have a strong influence, but this is very strongly modified by the ruling planet on the Ascendent. Also very strongly significant are the 'radix' (root positions at birth) of the planets in the houses. The combination of all these factors, which will balance together provide the key to an accurate assessment, and although there are many blind alleys, careful scrutiny, intelligent analysis and experience will reap their rewards and provide immense satisfaction.

Below: *An astrologer's study as can be seen from the instruments in the room and the ships which navigated by the stars through the window, and combining the function of astrologer and astronomer.*